AND THEN THERE'S THIS

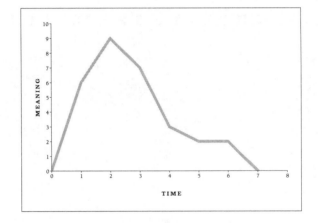

AND THEN THERE'S THIS

HOW STORIES LIVE AND DIE
IN VIRAL CULTURE

BILL WASIK

VIKING

VIKING
Published by the Penguin Group
Penguin Group (USA) Inc., 375 Hudson Street, New York, New York 10014, U.S.A. • Penguin
Group (Canada), 90 Eglinton Avenue East, Suite 700, Toronto, Ontario, Canada M4P 2Y3 (a di-
vision of Pearson Penguin Canada Inc.) • Penguin Books Ltd, 80 Strand, London WC2R 0RL,
England • Penguin Ireland, 25 St Stephen's Green, Dublin 2, Ireland (a division of Penguin
Books Ltd) • Penguin Books Australia Ltd, 250 Camberwell Road, Camberwell, Victoria
3124, Australia (a division of Pearson Australia Group Pty Ltd) • Penguin Books India Pvt
Ltd, 11 Community Centre, Panchsheel Park, New Delhi – 110 017, India • Penguin Group
(NZ), 67 Apollo Drive, Rosedale, North Shore 0632, New Zealand (a division of Pearson
New Zealand Ltd) • Penguin Books (South Africa) (Pty) Ltd, 24 Sturdee Avenue, Rosebank,
Johannesburg 2196, South Africa

Penguin Books Ltd, Registered Offices:
80 Strand, London WC2R 0RL, England

First published in 2009 by Viking Penguin,
a member of Penguin Group (USA) Inc.

1   3   5   7   9   10   8   6   4   2

Portions of this book first appeared in different form as "My Crowd" in Harper's Magazine and
"Hype Machine" in The Oxford American. "Hype Machine" was later published as "Annuals:
A North Carolina Band Navigates the Ephemeral Blogosphere" in Best Music Writing 2008,
edited by Nelson George and Daphne Carr (Da Capo Press).

Graphs by the author

Library of Congress Cataloging-in-Publication Data
Wasik, Bill.
And then there's this : how stories live and die in viral culture / Bill Wasik.
p.   cm.
Includes bibliographical references and index.
ISBN 978-0-670-02084-3
1. Internet—Social aspects.   2. Information society—Psychological aspects.
3. Internet users—Psychology.   4. Blogs—Social aspects.   I. Title.
HM851.W38 2009
303.48'33—dc22   2009004100

Printed in the United States of America
Set in ITC Berkeley Oldstyle Std with Barbera
Designed by Daniel Lagin

CONTENTS

INTRODUCTION:

KEY CONCEPTS

THE NANOSTORY

I begin with a plea to the future historians, those eminent and tenured minds of a generation as yet unconceived, who will sift through our benighted present, compiling its wreckage into wiki-books while lounging about in silvery bodysuits: to these learned men and women I ask only that in telling the story of this waning decade, the first of the twenty-first century, they will spare a thought for the fate of a girl named Blair Hornstine. Period photographs will record that Hornstine, as a high-school senior in the spring of 2003, was a small-framed girl with a full face, a sweep of dark, curly hair, and a broad, laconic smile. She was an outstanding student—the top of her high-school class in Moorestown, New Jersey, in fact, boasting a grade-point average of 4.689—and was slated to attend Harvard. But as her graduation neared, the district superintendent ruled that the second-place finisher, a boy whose almost-equal average (4.634) was lower due only to a technicality, should be allowed to share the valedictory honors.

At this point, the young Hornstine made a decision that even our future historians, no doubt more impervious than we to notions of the timeless or tragic, must rate almost as Sophoclean in the fatality of its folly. After learning of the superintendent's intention, Hornstine filed suit in U.S. federal court, demanding that she not only be named the sole valedictorian but also awarded punitive damages of $2.7 million. Incredibly, a U.S. district judge ruled in Hornstine's favor, giving her the top spot by fiat (though damages were later whittled down to only sixty grand). Meanwhile, however, a local paper for which she had written discovered that she was a serial plagiarist, having stolen sentences wholesale from such inadvisable marks as a think-tank report on arms control and a public address by President Bill Clinton. Harvard quickly rescinded its acceptance of Hornstine, who thereafter slunk away to a fate unknown.

I stoop to shovel up the remains of Blair Hornstine's reputation not to draw any moral from her misdeeds. Of the morals that might be drawn, roughly all were offered up at one point or another during the initial weeks after her lawsuit. She was "just another member of a hyper-accomplished generation for whom getting good grades and doing good deeds has become a way of life," wrote the *Los Angeles Times.* The *Philadelphia Daily News* eschewed such sociology, instead citing more structural causes: "With college costs skyrocketing, scholarship dollars limited and competition fierce for admissions, the road to the Ivy League has become a bloody battleground." MSNBC's Joe Scarborough declared that "across the country, parents are suing when the ball doesn't bounce their child's way," while CNN's Jeffrey Toobin went somewhat more Freudian, branding her judge father as another example of "lawyers. . . inflicting it on [their] children." Nonprofessional Internet pundits, meanwhile, were every bit as incisive. "The girl's father is a judge," wrote one proto-Toobin on MetaFilter, a popular community blog. "Guess he's taught her too much about the legal system." Echoed another commenter: "Behind every over-achieving student there are usually a pair of over-achieving parents who want their child to live up to their ridiculous expectations."

No, I offer up Blair Hornstine to history simply for the trajectory of her short-lived fame, the rapidity with which she was gobbled up into the mechanical maw of the national conversation, masticated thoroughly, and spat out:

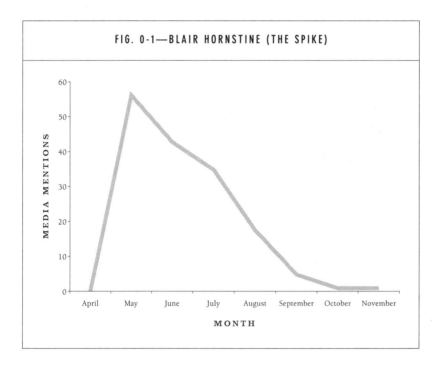

FIG. 0-1—BLAIR HORNSTINE (THE SPIKE)

This telltale spike, this ascent to sudden heights followed by a decline nearly as precipitous—it is a pattern that will recur throughout this book, and it is one that even the casual consumer of mass media will surely recognize. To keep up with current affairs today is to suffer under a terrible bombardment of Blair Hornstines, these media pile-ons that surge and die off within a matter of months, days, even hours. Consider just one of the weeks (May 25 through June 1) that Blair Hornstine was being dragged through the streets behind the media jeep; tied up beside her were a host of other persons or products or things, in various states of uptake or castoff—in the realm of politics, Pfc. Jessica Lynch (on her way down, as her rescue tale was found to have been exaggerated) and Howard Dean (on his way up in the race for president, having excited the Internet); in fashion, the trucker hat (on its way down) and Friendster.com (on its way up); in music, an indie-rock band called the Yeah Yeah Yeahs (down) and a new subgenre of "emo" called "screamo" (up); all these and more were experiencing their intense but ephemeral media moment during one week in the early summer of 2003.

We do not have an easy word to describe these transient bursts of attention, in part because we often categorize them differently based on their object. When this sort of fleeting attention attaches to things, we tend to call them "fads"; but this term, I think, conjures up too much the media-unsavvy consumer of an earlier era, while underestimating the extent to which our enthusiasms today are entirely knowing, postironic, *aware*. If there is one attribute of today's consumers, whether of products or of media, that differentiates them from their forebears of even twenty years ago, it is this: they are so acutely aware of how *media narratives themselves* operate, and of how their own behavior fits into these narratives, that their awareness feeds back almost immediately into their consumption itself.

Likewise, when this sort of transient attention falls on people, we tend to describe it as someone's "fifteen minutes of fame." But is celebrity really what is at work here? The majority of the tens of millions of people who pondered the story of Blair Hornstine never knew what she looked like, or cared. What they knew, instead, was how she fit handily into one or more of the various meanings imposed on her: the ambition-addled generation, the lawsuit-drunk society. Most people who remember Blair Hornstine today will recall her not by name or face but simply by role—as "that girl," perhaps, "who sued to become valedictorian." No name need even be invoked for her to do her conversational work.

In keeping with the entrepreneurial wordsmithery of the times, I would like to propose a new term to encompass all these miniature spikes, these vertiginous rises and falls: the *nanostory*. We allow ourselves to believe that a narrative is larger than itself, that it holds some portent for the long-term future; but soon enough we come to our senses, and the story, which cannot bear the weight of what we have heaped upon it, dies almost as suddenly as it was born. The gift we so graciously gave Blair Hornstine in 2003 was her fifteen minutes not of fame but of *meaning*.

VIRAL CULTURE

On May 27, 2003, during the same fitful weeks, I made up my mind to create a nanostory of my own. To sixty-three friends and acquaintances, I sent an e-mail that began as follows:

> You are invited to take part in MOB, the project that creates an inexplicable mob of people in New York City for ten minutes or less. Please forward this to other people you know who might like to join.

More precisely, I forwarded them this message, which, in order to conceal my identity as its original author, I had sent myself earlier that day from an anonymous webmail account. As further explanation, the e-mail offered a "frequently asked questions" (FAQ) section, which consisted of only one question:

> **Q. Why would I want to join an inexplicable mob?**
> A. Tons of other people are doing it.

Watches were to be synchronized against the U.S. government's atomic clocks, and the e-mail gave instructions for doing so. In order that the mob not form until the appointed time, participants were asked to approach the site from all four cardinal directions, based on birth month: January or July, up Broadway from the south; February or August, down Broadway from the north; etc. At 7:24 p.m. the following Tuesday—June 3—the mob was to converge upon Claire's Accessories, a small chain store near Astor Place that sold barrettes, scrunchies, and such. The gathering was to last for precisely seven minutes, until 7:31, at which time all would disperse. "NO ONE," the e-mail cautioned, "SHOULD REMAIN AT THE SITE AFTER 7:33."

My reason for sending this e-mail was simple: I was *bored*, by which I mean the world at that moment seemed adequate for neither my entertainment nor my sense of self. Something had to be done, and quickly. It was out of the question to undertake a project that might last, some new institution or some great work of art, for these would take time, exact cost, require risk, even as their odds for success hovered at nearly zero. Meanwhile, the odds of creating a short-lived sensation, of attracting incredible attention for a very brief period of time, were far more promising indeed. New York culture, like the national culture, was nothing but a shimmering cloud of nanostories, a churning constellation of "important" new bands and ideas and fashions that literally hundreds if not thousands of writers, in print and online, devoted themselves to building up and then dismantling with alacrity. I wanted my new project to be what someone would call "The X of the Summer," before I even contemplated exactly what X might be.

In the Internet, moreover, I had been handed a set of tools that allowed sensations to be created by anyone for almost no cost. Some of the successes had been epic, as in the case of *The Blair Witch Project*, which cost roughly $22,000 to make but earned, after a brilliant and dirt-cheap Internet marketing campaign, more than $248 million in gross—an anecdote that launched a thousand business books. (The sequel cost $15 million and flopped.) Scores of other viral victories had been considerably more modest financially but eye-opening nonetheless. A gregarious Turk named Mahir Çağrı lured literally millions of visitors to his slapdash personal home page, which professed his love for beautiful women and popularized, for most of a year, the greeting "I kiss you!" A twentysomething New Yorker named Jonah Peretti (who figures in chapter 3 of this book) sent to his friends an e-mail exchange he had had with Nike, and weeks later found that it had been disseminated to literally millions of people; he later went on to create more such "contagious media" projects and even taught a class on the subject at NYU. These sorts of links passed from person to person, from in-box to in-box, arriving once a week or even daily. Sometimes they were essentially found objects (like Mahir's home page), culled from the dark corners of the web in the service of semi-ironic hipster sport; but as the years went on, increasingly the forwarded e-mails linked to content that was consciously *made to spread*. The "viral," whether e-mail or website or song or video, was gradually emerging as a new genre of communication, even of art.

A marginal genre only a few years ago, the intentional viral has become central as this decade malingers on. Each day, hundreds of millions of videos are viewed on YouTube, and hundreds of thousands are uploaded. The viral currents charging through MySpace, with its millions of members and tens of thousands of bands, can literally create a number-one band—cf. the Arctic Monkeys—while the network of indie-rock music blogs, chief among them Pitchfork Media, is arguably the most important influence on which smaller bands prosper and which languish. Corporations are funneling million-dollar budgets into "word-of-mouth" marketing, with its emphasis on quick-hit pass-along ads, short-lived web "experiences," promotional blogs, and endless Internet tie-ins to the companies' more traditional campaigns. In national politics, the Internet has emerged as the crucial location for volunteer recruitment, fund-raising, and, above all, "conversation"—if one can accept that as a euphemism for the churning mess of interconnected blogs, most of them partisan, that every day and night are looking for opportunities to score political points against their enemies. The traditional media, unsure of their own business models, have moved to adapt, scrutinizing their most e-mailed lists for clues to the zeitgeist and then sending their reporters to chase the sorts of contagious stories that the Internet audience craves. All of this money and energy is aimed at creating hyperquick blowups, the kind of miniature crazes whose success is measured in hits and whose life span is measured in months if not weeks or days.

Sudden success has ever been the truest American dream, in 1800 and in 2000 and, God willing, in 2200, among those who survive the terror attacks and sea swells and oil wars. But what this particular decade, the first of the twenty-first century, has built, I would argue, is a new *viral culture* based on a new type of sudden success—a success with four key attributes. The first is outright speed: viral culture confers success with incredible rapidity, in a few weeks at the outside. The second is shamelessness: it is a success defined entirely by attention, and whether that attention is positive or negative matters hardly one bit. The third is duration: it is a success generally assumed to be ephemeral even by those caught up in it. These first three attributes, it should be noted, are simply more extreme versions of the overnight success afforded by television.

The fourth attribute, however, is new and somewhat surprising. It is what one might call sophistication: where TV success was a passive thing, success in viral culture is interactive, born of mass participation, defined by an awareness of the conditions of its creation. Viral culture is built, that is, upon what one might call the *media mind*.

THE MEDIA MIND

In the waning days of 2006, *Time* magazine blundered into ridicule by choosing "You" as its Person of the Year. On a CNN special, *Time* editor Richard Stengel announced the decision while brandishing a copy of the issue, whose cover's reflective Mylar panel served as a murky sort of mirror.

> STENGEL: *Time*'s 2006 person of the year is—*you!*
>
> SOLEDAD O'BRIEN: Literally me?
>
> STENGEL: Yes, you! Me! Everyone!

Just four weeks later the *New York Observer* would describe the choice as "a public belly flop, an instant punch line among readers and commentators"; and indeed, in their shared derision for *Time*, American pundits had come together in an almost touching moment of fellow feeling. From the right, Jonah Goldberg groused, "You are Person of the Year because the editors of *Time* want to live in a Feel-Good Age where everyone is empowered." From the left, Frank Rich bemoaned what You were ignoring: "In the Iraq era, the dropout nostrums of choice are not the drugs and drug culture of the Vietnam era but the equally self-gratifying and narcissistic (if less psychedelic) pastimes of the Internet." *Time* and its critics seemed strangely united, in fact, in their *interpretation* of the choice, and of the underlying online reality it was supposed to celebrate. "You" were supposed to have taken control of the culture—"the many wresting power from the few"—simply by enacting, each of you together, your naïve, untutored yearnings for community and self-expression. As NBC anchor Brian Williams put it, in a (cautionary) piece in *Time*'s package:

> The larger dynamic at work is the celebration of self. The implied message is that if it has to do with you, or your life, it's important

enough to tell someone. Publish it, record it . . . but for goodness'
sake, share it—get it out there so that others can enjoy it.

Let us set aside, for a moment, the irony of Brian Williams accusing
others of the "celebration of self," and let us instead pose a question:
does this vision of Internet culture—as a playground for unsophisti-
cated navel-gazers—actually square with reality? I would argue that it
is a deep misunderstanding, and one that dates from an earlier era.
Before the Internet, only professionals could attract audiences that
ranged far beyond their own circle of acquaintance. But today, we have
an era of truly popular culture that is not professionally created: people
can now attract tremendous followings for their writing or art (or
music, etc.) while making their livelihoods elsewhere. For this reason,
debates about the Internet's effect on culture tend necessarily to boil
down to debates over the merits of amateurism. Web 2.0 boosters celebrate the power of the collaborative many, who are breaking the grip
of the elites (and corporations) over the creation and distribution of
culture. Detractors fret that the rise of the amateur portends a decline
in quality, that a culture without professionals is a culture without
professionalism—a world of journalism without regard for fact, art without regard for craft, language without regard for grammar, and so on.

Mostly, though, both sides miss the point, because both lean, like
Williams, on a homespun notion of the "amateur" that simply doesn't
reflect how amateurs act when they get an audience online. The majority of bloggers may well be writing tedious personal journals, but the
readership of that kind of blog is usually not intended to stray, nor does
it stray in practice, beyond the bounds of the blogger's own acquaintance. Much the same can be said of YouTube or Flickr: the content is
purely personal and pedestrian precisely to the extent that its poster
cares nothing for attracting an audience. With rare exceptions, purely
personal content posted on the Internet simply doesn't matter to anyone
its creator doesn't know, any more than would the diary on your own

nightstand. Surely *Time* would never have named "You" the person of the year if all blogs were diaries, if all YouTube videos were bedroom soliloquies.

Bloggers, mashup artists, YouTube videographers, political "hacktivists"—these people aren't sitting in their bedrooms spinning out moony personal diaries, hoping that someone will come along and recognize them. Aware they're always being watched, they act accordingly, tailoring their posts to draw traffic, stirring up controversy, watching their stats to see what works and what doesn't. They develop a meta-understanding of the conversation they're in and how that conversation works, and they try to figure out where it's going so they can get there first. Often these web amateurs have learned these rules just by observing—by lurking on other blogs before starting their own, for example. But just as often they learn from on-the-job experience of sorts, by having scores of ideas fail while one succeeds against all expectation. Either way, countless Internet "amateurs" come to think about their projects with a hard-nosed sophistication that rivals anything to be found inside the conference rooms of our corporate culturemasters.

In fact, the relevant actors of so-called consumer-generated media—the tens if not hundreds of thousands of content creators who are attracting fans beyond their own circles of friends—are every bit as savvy, as ambitious, and as calculating as aspiring culture-makers have ever been. *Time*'s own examples bore this out: the amateurs who won a following that year invariably had done so cannily. S. R. Sidarth, the young man responsible for Sen. George Allen's infamous "macaca" moment on YouTube, was an ambitious young volunteer for the opposing campaign who was trailing Allen specifically to document his missteps. The Silence Xperiment, a pseudonymous "bedroom producer" who created a wildly popular mashup album combining the raps of 50 Cent with the music of Queen, had previously DJed clubs, and also had his own radio show (albeit at a college station). Lane Hudson, the blogger whose "Stop Sex Predators" blog posted the e-mails and chats that brought down Rep. Mark Foley, himself worked for a number of political campaigns, including John Kerry's for president. Tila Tequila, the model/singer who became the first MySpace phenomenon, sent a mass e-mail to "30,000 to 50,000" people inviting them to join up and add her as a friend. These were people who wanted a piece of mass culture; and so they watched the culture, learned from the culture, and then used what they learned to get what they wanted.

And so it goes every year, with the hordes of supposed naïfs out there writing their blogs, producing their videos, posting their songs. Bands trawl other bands' MySpace pages, raiding their friend lists to try to find potential fans for themselves; every month, thousands more buy a software program called Easy Adder, which (for $24.95) allows them to automate the friend-request process, sending friend requests to hundreds or even thousands of potential friends at a time. On YouTube, video-makers create their own "channels" with customizable promotional backdrops, and they pimp their home page URLs at the ends of videos. Bloggers follow their stats and trackbacks; they add other bloggers to their "blogrolls" in hopes they will reciprocate. Having been sold culture for so many years, in so many sophisticated ways, consumers have now been handed the tools to *sell themselves* and they are doing so with great gusto.

All this is why I, for one, had no quibble with *Time*'s choice of "You" as the person of the year. Indeed, I will happily put "You" forward as the defining person of this whole random decade, which our hordes of cultural critics have redefined so often and so variously that it lacks an identity or even a name (the Zeros? the Oughties?). But make no mistake: I am onto You. You are no more starry-eyed about community and collaboration and "people power" and self-expression than is Brian Williams or Jonah Goldberg or Frank Rich; no more, for that matter, than am I. You blog and photograph and record precisely so you can be read and heard and seen by others. You monitor and you scheme and you promote, just like the hit-addled corporate culture has been teaching you for years. Because when your words or actions or art are available not only to your friends but to potentially thousands or even millions of strangers, it changes what you say, how you act, how you see yourself. You become aware of yourself as a character on a stage, as a public figure with a meaning. You develop, that is, the *media mind*. You know exactly what you are doing.

THE EXPERIMENTAL METHOD

"If you can measure it, you can manage it," I heard a man behind the podium at a marketing conference say. He attributed this remark to the late-nineteenth-century scientist and engineer Lord Kelvin—whom he called "a pretty big data geek himself, back in the day"—but added, "The quote is actually much more Old English than that." The full quote, as it happens, takes as its subject not management but science itself, and it is much beloved of scientists, appearing on some fifteen thousand different websites in its original not-quite-Old-English, which reads as follows:

> I often say that when you can measure what you are speaking about, and express it in numbers, you know something about it; but when you cannot measure it, when you cannot express it in numbers, your knowledge is of a meagre and unsatisfactory kind; it may be the beginning of knowledge, but you have scarcely in your thoughts advanced to the state of *Science*, whatever the matter may be.

Kelvin's point is that data is a necessary undergirding of science—indeed, data *engenders* science. And this is a crucial insight to understanding viral culture. For the better part of a century, corporations have seen culture through a lens of numbers, from 1926, when Maxwell

Sackheim invented the Book-of-the-Month Club and began the hard-ening of the art of direct marketing into a statistical science; to 1936, when George Gallup used a scientifically selected random sample to correctly call the presidential election for FDR; to 1941, when the soci-ologist Robert Merton convened the first "focus group," a tool that mar-keters would quickly use to wed the wisdom of polling to the qualitative insights of small-group conversations; and so on into the rest of the century, with its Nielsen ratings and demographic profiling and direct marketing. Corporate America has had the numbers and has used them to conduct its profit-seeking experiments on all of us.

But the Internet is revolutionary in how it has democratized not just culture-making but *culture monitoring,* giving individual creators a profusion of data with which to identify trends surrounding their own work and that of others. On YouTube, a video's poster—or anyone else who cares to check—is privy to the kind of internals that TV execu-tives can only dream of: not just real-time rankings of how often a video has been viewed, but which other videos a fan is likely to enjoy as well, based on the behavior of other users. For music, the story is the same: on MySpace, a band can track which of its songs are downloaded more and how this compares to other bands. This shift has seeped into the old media as well—writers for print newspapers or magazines, through their site's "most e-mailed" lists, can see precisely which of their articles attain the heights of ubiquity and which fall into oblivion. If one's built-in numbers do not provide enough market intelligence, there are countless other sites to consult. How many bloggers have linked to your site? The search engine Technorati will tell you, and also show you what those bloggers have to say. How is your site doing versus the competition? At Alexa.com you can see not only your site's rank in its category but also plot it against other sites you choose.

This glut of data, combined with the ability to assume anonymity or pseudonymity—i.e., to act without one's identity influencing the re-sults, which is another crucial prerequisite of science—is establishing the Internet as an unprecedented medium for cultural *experimentation*. As more and more Americans become aware of the patterns and forces that shape culture, they begin to develop their own hypotheses about what will spread and what won't. Online, with minimal cost or risk, they can test these theories, tweaking different versions of their would-be viral projects and monitoring the results, which in turn feed back into how future projects are made. In viral culture, we are all driven by the ratings, the numbers, the Internet equivalent of the box-office gross.

It is with trembling anticipation that I welcome our new generation of cultural scientists, to whom I dedicate this book and for whom I hope it might serve as both primer and cautionary tale. In its pages I survey the various precincts of viral culture, from politics and litera-ture to marketing and music, in locales throughout the virtual world (blogs, chat rooms, MySpace, YouTube) and the real one (New York, Washington, Minneapolis, Santa Monica). In each chapter, I also detail the results of one of my own admittedly modest experiments in viral culture. But before those nanostories can be told, I need to return to that e-mail of May 27, 2003, and reveal what it portended for Claire's Accessories, and for me.

1.

MY CROWD

EXPERIMENT:
THE MOB PROJECT

BOREDOM

I started the Mob Project because I was bored, I wrote above, and perhaps that explanation seems simple enough. But before we proceed to
the rise and fall of my peculiar social experiment, I think that boredom
is worth interrogating in some detail. The first recorded use of the term,
per the *OED*, did not take place until 1852, in Charles Dickens's *Bleak
House*, chapter 12. It is deployed by way of describing Lady Dedlock, a
woman with whose habits of mind I often find myself in sympathy:

> Concert, assembly, opera, theatre, drive, nothing is new to my
> Lady, under the worn-out heavens. Only last Sunday, when poor
> wretches were gay—. . . encompassing Paris with dancing, love-
> making, wine-drinking, tobacco-smoking, tomb-visiting, bil-
> liard, card and domino playing, quack-doctoring, and much
> murderous refuse, animate and inanimate—only last Sunday,

my Lady, in the desolation of Boredom and the clutch of Giant Despair, almost hated her own maid for being in spirits.

Psychologists have been trying to elucidate the nature of boredom since at least Sigmund Freud, who identified a "lassitude" in young women that he attributed to penis envy. In 1951, Otto Fenichel described boredom as a state where the "drive-tension" is present but the "drive-aim" is absent, a state of mind that he said could be "schematically formulated" in this enigmatic but undeniably evocative way: "I am excited. If I allow this excitation to continue I shall get anxious. Therefore I tell myself, I am not at all excited, I don't want to do anything. Simultaneously, however, I feel I do want to do something; but I have forgotten my original goal and do not know what I want to do. The external world must do something to relieve me of my tension without making me anxious."

In the 1970s, researchers developed various tests designed, in part, to assess the boredom-plagued, from the Imaginal Processes Inventory (Singer and Antrobus, 1970) to the Sensation Seeking Scale (Zuckerman, Eysenck & Eysenck, 1978). But it was not until 1986, with the unveiling of the Boredom Proneness Scale (BPS), that the propensity toward boredom in the individual could be comprehensively measured and reckoned with. The test was created by Richard Farmer and Norman Sundberg, both of the University of Oregon, and it has allowed researchers in the two decades since to tally up boredom's grim wages. The boredom-prone, we have discovered, display higher rates of procrastination, inattention, narcissism, poor work performance, and "solitary sexual behaviors" including both onanism and the resort to pornography.

The BPS test consists of twenty-eight statements to which respondents answer true or false, with a point assessed for each boredom-aligned choice, e.g.:

1. *It is easy for me to concentrate on my activities.* [+1 for False.]
5. *I am often trapped in situations where I have to do meaningless things.* [+1 for True.]
25. *Unless I am doing something exciting, even dangerous, I feel half-dead and dull.* [+1 for True.]

Farmer and Sundberg found the average score to be roughly 10. My own score is 16, and indeed when I peruse the list of correct answers I feel as if I am scanning a psychological diagnosis of myself. I *do* find it hard to concentrate; I *do* find myself constantly trapped doing meaningless things; and half-dead or dull does not begin to describe how I feel when I lack a project that is adequately transgressive or, worse, find myself exiled somewhere among the slow-witted. I worry about other matters while I work (#2), and I find that time passes slowly (#3). I am bad at waiting patiently (#15), and in fact when I am forced to wait in line, I get restless (#17). Even for those questions to which I give the allegedly nonbored answer, I tend to feel I am forfeiting the points on some technicality. Yes, I do have "projects in mind, all the time" (#7)— so many that few of them ever get acted upon, precisely because my desperate craving for variety means that I am rarely satisfied for very long with even projects that are hypothetical. Yes, others do tend to say that I am a "creative or imaginative person" (#22), but honestly I think this is due to declining standards.

And no, I do not often find myself "at loose ends" (#4), sitting around doing nothing (#14), with "time on my hands" (#16), without "something to do or see to keep me interested" (#13). But such has been true for me only since the start of this viral decade, when my idle stretches have been erased by the grace of the Internet, with its soothingly fast and infinitely available distractions, engaging me for hours on end without assuaging my fundamental boredom in any way. In fact, I would advance the prediction that answers to these latter four questions have become meaningless in recent years, when all of our interactive technologies—video games and mobile devices as well as the web—have kept those of us most boredom-prone from generally thinking, as we might while watching TV, that we are "doing nothing," even if in every practical sense we are doing precisely that. I fear I am ahead of the science, however, because I have been unable to find any study that either supports or undercuts this conjecture. I put the question to Richard Farmer, the lead author of the Boredom Proneness Scale, only to find that he had not done boredom research in many years. He had moved on to other topics. I did not ask him why, though I have the glimmer of a notion.

EXPERIMENT: THE MOB PROJECT

That May my boredom was especially acute, but none of the projects crowding around in my mind seemed feasible. I wanted to use e-mail to get people to come to some sort of show, where something surprising would happen, perhaps involving a fight; or an entire fake arts scene, maybe, some tight-knit band of fictitious young artists and writers who all lived together in a loft, and we would reel in journalists and would-be admirers eager to congratulate themselves for having discovered the next big thing. Both of these ideas seemed far too difficult. It was while ruminating on these two ideas, in the shower, that I realized I needed to make my idea *lazier*. I could use e-mail to gather an audience for a show, yes, but the point of the show should be no show at all: the e-mail would be straightforward about exactly what people would see, namely nothing but *themselves,* coming together for no reason at all. Such a project would work, I reflected, because it was *meta,* i.e., it was a self-conscious idea for a self-conscious culture, a promise to create something out of nothing. It was the perfect project for me.

During the week between the first MOB e-mail and the appointed day, I found myself anxious, not knowing what to expect. MOB's only goal was to attract a crowd, but as an event it had none of the typical draws: no name of any artist or performer, no endorsement by any noted tastemaker. All it had was its own ironically wild, unsupportable claims—that "tons" of people would be there, that they would constitute a "mob." The subject heading of the e-mail had read *MOB #1*, so as to imply that it was the first in what would be an ongoing series of gatherings. (In fact, I was unsure whether there would be a MOB #2.) As I was gathering my things to head north the seven blocks from my office to the mob site, I received a call from my friend Eugene, a stand-up comedian whose attitude toward daily living I have long admired. Once, on a slow day while he was working at an ice-cream store, he slid a shovel through the inside handles of the store's plate-glass front doors, along with a note that read CLOSED DUE TO SHOVEL.

"Is the mob supposed to be at Claire's Accessories?" Eugene asked.

Yes, I said.

"There's six cops standing guard in front of it," he said. "And a paddywagon."

This was not the mob I had been anticipating. If anyone was to land in that paddywagon, I thought, it ought to be me, and so I hastened to the site. The cops, thankfully, did not seem to be in an arresting mood. But they would not allow anyone to enter the store, even when we told them (not unpersuasively, I thought) that we were desperate accessories shoppers. I scanned the faces of passersby, hoping to divine how many had come to mob—quite a few, I judged, based on their excited yet wry expressions, but seeing the police they understandably hurried past. Still others lingered around, filming with handheld video cameras or snapping digital pictures. A radio crew lurked with a boom mike. Despite the police, my single e-mail had generated enough steam to power a respectable spectacle.

The underlying science of the Mob Project seemed sound, and so I readied plans for MOB #2, which would be held two weeks later, on

June 17. I found four ill-frequented bars near the intended site and had the participants gather at those beforehand, again split by the month of their birth. Ten minutes before the appointed time of 7:27 p.m., slips of paper bearing the final destination were distributed at the bars. The site was the Macy's rugs department, which in that tremendous store is a mysterious and inaccessible kingdom, the farthest reach of the ninth and uppermost floor, accessed by a seemingly endless series of ancient escalators that grind past women's apparel and outerwear and furs and fine china and the in-store Starbucks and Au Bon Pain. By quarter past seven waves of mobbers were sweeping through the dimly illuminated furniture department, glancing sidelong toward the rugs room as they pretended to shop for loveseats and bureaus; but all at once, in a giant rush, two hundred people wandered over to the carpet in the back left corner and, as instructed, informed clerks that they all lived together in a Long Island City commune and were looking for a "love rug."

E-MAIL MOB TAKES MANHATTAN read the headline two days later on *Wired News*, an online technology-news site. More media took note, and interview requests began to filter in to my anonymous webmail account: on June 18, from *New York Magazine*; on June 20, from the *New York Observer*, NPR's *All Things Considered*, the BBC World Service, the Italian daily *Corriere della Serra*. By MOB #3, which was held two weeks after the previous one, I had gotten fifteen requests in total. Would-be mobbers in other cities had heard the call as well, and soon I received e-mails from San Francisco, Minneapolis, Boston, Austin, announcing their own local chapters. Some asked for advice, which I very gladly gave. ("Before you send out the instructions, visit the spot at the same time and on the same day of the week, and figure out how long it will take people to get to the mob spot, etc.," I wrote to Minneapolis.)

Perhaps most important, the Mob Project was almost immediately taken up by blogs. A blog called Cheesebikini, run by a thirty-one-year-old graduate student in Berkeley named Sean Savage, gave the concept its name—"flash mobs"—as an homage to a 1973 science-fiction short story called "Flash Crowd," by Larry Niven. The story is a warning about the unexpected downside of cheap teleportation technology: packs of thrill seekers can beam themselves in whenever something exciting is going down. The protagonist, Jerryberry Jensen, is a TV journalist who broadcasts a fight in a shopping mall, which soon, thanks to teleportation booths, grows into a multiday riot, with miscreants beaming in from around the world. Jensen is blamed, and his bosses threaten to fire him, but eventually he clears his name by showing how the technology was to blame. Since the mid-1990s, the term "flash crowd" had been invoked from time to time as a metaphor for the sudden and debilitating traffic surges that can occur when a small website is linked to by a very popular one. This is more commonly known as the "Slashdot effect," after the popular tech-head site Slashdot.org, which was—and still is—known to choke the sites on which it bestows links.

With its meteorological resonance, its evocation of a "flash flood" of people mobbing a place or a site or a thing all at once and then dispersing, the term "flash mob" was utterly perfect. The phenomenon it described, now properly named, could venture out into the universe and begin swiftly, stylishly, assuredly to multiply.

HYPOTHESIS

The logic behind the Mob Project ran, roughly, as follows.

1. At any given time in New York—or in any other city where culture is actively made—the vast majority of events (concerts, plays, readings, comedy nights, and gallery shows, but also protests, charities, association meetings) are summarily ignored, while a small subset of events attracts enormous audiences and, soon, media attention.

2. For most of these latter events, the beneficiaries of that ineffable boon known as *buzz,* one can, after the fact, point out nominal reasons for their sudden popularity: high quality, for example; or perception of high quality due to general acclamation, or at least an assumption of general acclamation; or the participation of some well-liked figure, or the presence, or rumored presence, of same; etc.

3. *But:* so often does popularity, even among the highest of brow, bear no relationship to merit, that an experiment might be devised to determine just how far one might take the former while neglecting the latter entirely; that is, how much buzz one could create about an event whose only point was buzz, a show whose audience was itself the only show. Given all culture in New York was demonstrably commingled with *scenesterism,* my thinking ran, it should theoretically be possible to create an art project consisting of *pure scene*—meaning the scene would be the entire point of the work, and indeed would itself constitute the work.

At its best, the Mob Project brought to this task a sort of formal unity, as can be illustrated in MOB #3, which took place fifteen days after #2. To get the slips with the destination, invitees were required to roam the downstairs food court of Grand Central Station, looking for Mob Project representatives reading the *New York Review of Books.* The secret location was a hotel adjacent to the station on Forty-second Street, the Grand Hyatt, which has a block-long lobby with fixtures in the high '80s style: gold-chrome railings and sepia-mirror walls and a fountain in marblish stone and a mezzanine overhead, ringed around. Mob time was set for 7:07 p.m., the tail end of the evening rush hour; the train station next door was thick with commuters and so (visible through the hotel's tinted-glass facade) was the sidewalk outside, but the lobby was nearly empty: only a few besuited types, guests presumably, sunk here and there into armchairs.

Starting five minutes beforehand the mob members slipped in, in twos and threes and tens, milling around in the lobby and making stylish small talk. Then all at once, they rode the elevators and escalators up to the mezzanine and wordlessly lined the banister, like so:

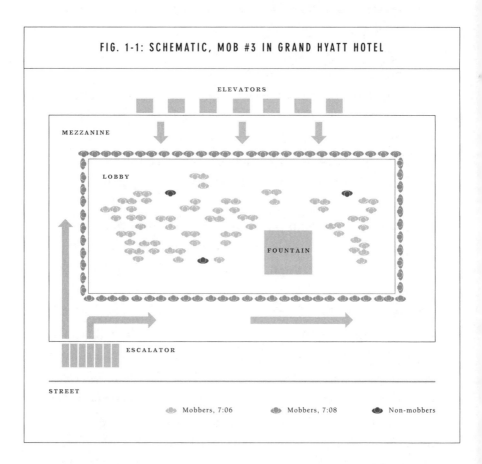

FIG. 1-1: SCHEMATIC, MOB #3 IN GRAND HYATT HOTEL

The handful of hotel guests were still there, alone again, except now they were confronted with a hundreds-strong armada of mobbers overhead, arrayed shoulder to shoulder, staring silently down. Intimidation was not the point; we were staring down at *where we had just been,* and also across at one another, two hundred artist-spectators commandeering an atrium on Forty-second Street as a coliseum-style theater of self-regard. After five minutes of staring, the ring erupted into precisely fifteen seconds of tumultuous applause—for itself—after which it scattered back downstairs and out the door, just as the police cruisers were rolling up, flashers on.

THE MEME, SUPREME

From the moment flash mobs first began to spread, there was a term applied to them by both boosters and detractors, and that term was *meme.* "The Flash Mob meme is #1 with a bullet," wrote the author Howard Rheingold on his blog. Three days later, on MetaFilter, one commenter wrote, "I was going to take the time to savage this wretched warmed-over meme, but am delighted to see that so many of you have already done so"; countered the next commenter, "I happen to think the meme is a bit silly, but the backlash even more so." In September, when the comic strip *Doonesbury* had one of its characters create flash mobs for Howard Dean, one blogger named Eric enthused, "Trust Gary [*sic*] Trudeau to combine the hottest memes of the summer," adding as an aside: "Yes, I fully realize that [I] just called Dr Dean a meme."

Readers will be excused for their ignorance of this term, though in 1998 it did enter the Merriam-Webster dictionary, which defines it as "an idea, behavior, style, or usage that spreads from person to person within a culture." The operative word here is "spreads," for this simple monosyllabic noun has buried within it a particular vision of culture and how it evolves. In a meme's-eye view of the world, any idea—from a religious belief or a political affiliation to a new style of jeans or a catchy tune—can be seen as a sort of independent agent loosed into the population, where it travels from mind to mind, burrowing into each, colonizing all as widely and ruthlessly as it can. Some brains are more susceptible than others to certain memes, but by and large memes spread by virtue of their own inherent contagiousness. The meme idea, that is, sees cultural entities as being similar to genes, or better, to *viruses,* and in fact the term "viral" is often used to express the same idea.

If we consider the meme idea itself as a meme, we see that its virulence in the Internet era has been impressive. The term was coined in 1976 by the biologist Richard Dawkins in his first book, *The Selfish Gene,* in which he persuasively argues that genes are the operative subjects of evolutionary selection: that is, individuals struggle first and foremost to perpetuate their genes, and insofar as evolution is driven by the "survival of the fittest," it is the fitness of our genes, not of us, that is the relevant factor. He puts forward a unified vision of history in which replication is king: in Dawkins's view, from that very first day when, somewhere in the murk, there emerged the first genes—molecules with the ability to create copies of themselves— these selfish replicators have been orchestrating the whole shebang. After extending out this argument to explain the evolution of species, Dawkins turns to the question of human culture. If replication, over long periods of time, explains why we exist, then might it not serve also to explain what inhabits our minds? Dawkins writes, with characteristic flourish,

> I think that a new kind of replicator has recently emerged on this very planet. It is staring us in the face. It is still in its infancy, still drifting clumsily about in its primeval soup. . . . The new soup is the soup of human culture. We need a name for the new replicator, a noun that conveys the idea of a unit of cultural transmission, or a unit of imitation. "Mimeme" [Greek for "that which is imitated"] comes from a suitable Greek root, but I want a mono-

syllable that sounds a bit like gene. I hope my classicist friends
will forgive me if I abbreviate mimeme to *meme*.

Although Dawkins clearly intends the meme to be analogous first
and foremost to the gene—which spreads itself only through succes-
sive generations, through the reproduction of its host—on the very
same page he invokes the more apt biological metaphor of the virus.
"When you plant a fertile meme in my mind you literally parasitize my
brain," he wrote, "turning it into a vehicle for the meme's propagation
in just the way that a virus may parasitize the genetic mechanism of a
host cell."

Why has the meme meme spread? Why has the viral become so viral?
The Selfish Gene was a bestselling book thirty years ago, but it was not
until the mid-1990s that the meme and viral ideas became epidemics of
their own. I would hazard two reasons for this chronology, one psychological and one technological. The psychological reason is the rise of
market consciousness, in a culture where stock ownership increased
during the 1990s from just under a quarter to more than half. After all,
the meme vision of culture—where ideas compete for brain space, un-
burdened by history or context—really resembles nothing so much as
an economist's dream of the free market. We are asked to admire the
marvelous theoretical efficiencies (no barriers to entry, unfettered competition, persistence of the fittest) but to ignore the factual inequalities:
the fact, for example, that so many of our most persistent memes succeed only through elaborate sponsorship (what would be a genetic analogy here? factory-farm breeding, perhaps?), while other, fitter memes
wither.

The other, technological reason for the rise of the meme/viral idea
is perhaps more obvious: the Internet. But it is worth teasing out just
what about the Internet has conjured up these memes all around us.
Yes, the Internet allows us to communicate instantaneously with others

around the world, but that has been possible since the telegraph. Yes, the Internet allows us to find others with similar interests and chat among ourselves; but this is just an online analogue of what we always have been able to do in person, even if perhaps not on such a large scale. What the Internet has done to change culture—to create a new, viral culture—is to *archive* trillions of our communications, to make them linkable, trackable, searchable, quantifiable, so they can serve as ready grist for yet more conversation. In an offline age, we might have had a vague notion that a slang phrase or a song or a perception of a product or an enthusiasm for a candidate was spreading through social groups; but lacking any hard data about *how* it was spreading, why would any of us (aside from marketers and sundry social scientists) really care? Today, though, in the Internet, we have a trillion-terabyte answer that in turn has influenced our questions. We can see how we are embedded in numerical currents, how we precede or lag curves, how we are enmeshed in so-called social networks, and how our networks compare to the networks of others. The Internet has given us not just new ways of communicating but new ways of measuring ourselves.

PROPAGATION

To spread the Mob Project, I endeavored to devise a *media strategy* on the project's own terms. The mob was all about the herd instinct, I reasoned, about the desire not to be left out of the latest fad; logically, then, it should grow as quickly as possible, and eventually—this seemed obvious—to buckle under the weight of its own popularity. I developed a simple maxim for myself, as custodian of the mob: "Anything that grows the mob is pro-mob." And in accordance with this principle, I gave interviews to all reporters who asked. In the six weeks following MOB #3 I did perhaps thirty different interviews, not only with local newspapers (the *Post* and the *Daily News*, though not yet the

Times—more on that later) but also with *Time, Time Out New York*, the *Christian Science Monitor*, the *San Francisco Chronicle*, the *Chicago Tribune*, the Associated Press, Reuters, Agence France-Presse, and countless websites.

There was also the matter of how I would be identified. My original preference had been to remain entirely anonymous, but I had only half succeeded; at the first, aborted mob, a radio reporter had discovered my first name and broadcast it, and so I was forced to be Bill—or, more often, "Bill"—in my dealings with the media thereafter. "[L]ike Cher and Madonna, prefers to use only his first name," wrote the *Chicago Daily Herald*. (To those who asked my occupation, I replied simply that I worked in the "culture industry.") Usually a flash-mob story would invoke me roughly three quarters of the way down, as the "shadowy figure" at the center of the project. There were dark questions as to my intentions. "Bill, who denies he is on a power-trip, declined to be identified," intoned Britain's *Daily Mirror*. Here is an exchange from Fox News's *On the Record with Greta Van Susteren*:

ANCHOR: Now, the guy who came up with the Mob Project is a mystery man named Bill. Do either of you know who he is?
MOBBER ONE: Nope.
MOBBER TWO: Well, I've—I've e-mailed him. That's about it.
MOBBER ONE: Oh, you have . . . ?
ANCHOR: What—what—who is this Bill? Do you know anything about him?
MOBBER TWO: Well, from what I've read, he's a—he works in the culture industry, and that's—that's about as specific as we've gotten with him.

As the media frenzy over the mobs grew, so did the mobs themselves. For MOB #4, I sent the mob to a shoe store in SoHo, a spacious plate-glassed corner boutique whose high ceilings and walls made of undulating mosaic gave it an almost aquatic feel, and I was astonished to see the mob assemble: as I marched with one strand streaming down Lafayette, we saw another mounting a pincers movement around Prince Street from the east, pouring in through the glass doors past the agape mouths of the attendants, perhaps three hundred bodies, packing the space and then, once no one else could enter, crowding around the sidewalk, everyone gawking, taking pictures with cameras, calling friends on cell phones (as the instructions for this mob had ordered), each pretending to be a tourist, all feigning awe—an awe I myself truly felt— to be not merely in New York but so close to the center of something so big.

Outside New York, too, the mob was multiplying in dizzying ways, far past the point that I could correspond with the leaders or even keep up with all the different new cities: not only all across the United States but London, Vienna, twenty-one different municipalities in Germany. In July, soon after New York's MOB #4, Rome held its first two flash mobs; in the first, three hundred mobbers strode into a bookstore and demanded nonexistent titles (e.g., *Pinocchio 2: The Revenge*), while the second (which, based on descriptions I read later, is perhaps my favorite flash mob of any ever assembled) was held right in the Piazza dell'Esquilino, in a crosswalk just in front of the glorious Basilica di Santa Maria Maggiore, where the crowd broke into two and balletically crossed back and forth and met each other multiple times, first hugging, then fighting, and then asking for the time: *"CHE ORE SONO?"* yelled one semi-mob, and the other replied, *"LE SETTE E QUARANTA"*— "It's 7:40"—which, in fact, it was exactly.

UP: THE BANDWAGON EFFECT

When a British art magazine asked me who, among artists past or present, had most influenced the flash-mob project, I named Stanley

Milgram—i.e., the social psychologist best known for his authority experiments in which he induced average Americans to give seemingly fatal shocks to strangers. As it happens, I later discovered that Milgram also did a project much like a flash mob, in which a "stimulus crowd" of his confederates, varying in number from one to fifteen, stopped on a busy Manhattan sidewalk and all at once looked up to the same sixth-floor window. The results, in a chart from his paper "Notes on the Drawing Power of Crowds of Different Size":

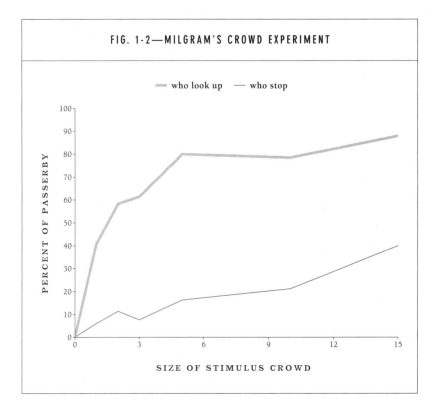

FIG. 1-2—MILGRAM'S CROWD EXPERIMENT

In this single chart, Milgram elegantly documented the essence of herd behavior, what economists call a "bandwagon effect": the instinctive tendency of the human animal to rely on the actions of others in choosing its own course of action. We get interested in the things we see others getting interested in. *Homo sapiens* has been jumping on bandwagons, as the expression goes, since long before the vogue for such vehicles in the late nineteenth century (when less popular American politicians would clamor to be seen aboard the bandwagon of a more popular candidate for another office, hence the meaning we have today); since long before, even, the invention of the wheel.

The bandwagon effect is especially pronounced in Internet culture-making, however, because popularity can immediately be factored into how choices are presented to us. If in our nonwired lives we jump on a bandwagon once a day, in our postwired existence we hop whole fleets of them—often without even knowing it. Start, for example, where most of us start online, with Google: when we search for a phrase, Google's sophisticated engine delivers our results in an order determined (at least in part) by how many searchers before us eventually clicked on the pages in question. Whenever we click on a top-ten Google result, we are jumping on an invisible bandwagon. Similarly with retailers such as Amazon, whose front-page offerings, tailored to each customer, are based on what other customers have bought: another invisible bandwagon. Then there are the countless visible bandwagons, in the form of the ubiquitous lists: most bought, most downloaded, most e-mailed, most linked-to. Even the august *New York Times*, through its "most e-mailed" list, has turned the news into a popularity contest, whose winners in turn get more attention among Internet readers who have only a limited amount of attention to give. Thus do the attention-rich invariably get richer.

In some cases, our bandwagons—online or off—do us a service, by weeding out extraneous or undesirable information through the "wisdom of crowds" (as a bestselling book by James Surowiecki put it). Moreover, in the case of culture, what is already popular in some respect has more intrinsic value: we read news, or watch television, or listen to music in part so we can have discussions with other people who have done the same. But it is a severe mistake to assume, as the economically minded often do, that the bandwagon effect manages to select for intrinsic worth, or even to give individuals what they actually want. This was demonstrated ingeniously a few years ago in an experiment run by Matthew Salganik, a sociologist who was then at Columbia University. Fourteen thousand participants were invited to join a music network where they could listen to songs, rate them, and, if they wanted, download the songs for free. A fifth of the volunteers—the "independent" group—were left entirely to their own tastes, unable to see what their fellows were downloading. The other four-fifths were split up into eight different networks—the "influence" groups—all of which saw the same songs, but listed in rank order based on how often they had been downloaded in that particular group. The songs were by almost entirely unknown bands, to avoid having songs get popular based on preexisting associations with the band's name.

What Salganik and his colleagues found was that the "independent" group chose songs that differed significantly from those chosen in the "influence" groups, which in turn differed significantly from one another. In their paper, the sociologists call the eight different networks "worlds," and they mean this in the philosophical sense of possible worlds: each network began from the same starting point with the same universe of songs, but each of these independent evolutionary environments yielded very different outcomes. A band called 52metro, for example, was #1 in one world but didn't even rate the top ten in five of the other seven worlds. Similarly, a band called Silent Film topped one chart but was #3, #4, #7, or #8 (twice) on five of the charts, and was entirely left off the other two. "Quality"—if we define that to mean the independent group's choices—did not seem to be entirely irrelevant: the top-rated song on their list, by a group called Parker Theory, made all eight of the "influence" lists and topped five of them. But of the other nine acts on the independent list, one was entirely shut out of the influence lists, and three made only two lists. On average, the top ten bands for the independent group made only four of the eight influence lists. Apparently they were drowned out, in the other worlds, by noise from the bandwagons.

The Mob Project was a *self-conscious* bandwagon—it advertised itself as a bandwagon, as a joke about conformity, and it lampooned bandwagons in doing so. But curiously, this seemed not to diminish its actual bandwagonesque properties. Indeed, if anything, the self-consciousness made it even more viral. The e-mails poured in: "I WANT IN." "Request to mob, sir." "Girls can keep secrets!" "Want to get my mob on." In Boston's first flash mob, entitled "Ode to Bill," hundreds packed the greeting-card aisles of a Harvard Square department store, telling bystanders who inquired that they were looking for a card for their "friend Bill in New York." By making a halfhearted, jesting attempt to elevate me to celebrity status, Boston had given the flash-mob genre an appropriately sly turn.

PEAK AND BACKLASH

The best attended of all the New York gatherings was MOB #6, which for a few beautiful minutes stifled what has to be the most ostentatious chain store in the entire city: the Times Square Toys "Я" Us, whose excesses are too many to catalog here but include, in the store's foyer, an actual operational Ferris wheel some sixty feet in diameter. Up until the appointed time of 7:18 p.m. the mobbers loitered on the upper level, among the GI Joes and the Nintendos and up inside the glittering pink of the two-floor Barbie palace. But then all at once the mob, five hundred strong, crowded around the floor's centerpiece, a life-size animatronic Tyrannosaurus rex that growls and feints with a Hollywood-class lifelikeness. "Fill in all around it," the mob slip had instructed. "It is like a terrible god to you."

Two minutes later, the mob dropped to its knees, moaning and cowering at the beast behind outstretched hands; in doing so we repaid this spectacle, which clearly was the product of not only untold expenditure but many man-months of *imagineering,* with an en masse enactment of the very emotions—visceral fright and infantile fealty—that it obviously had been designed to evoke. MOB #6 was, as many bloggers pointed out pejoratively, "cute," but the cuteness had been massed, refracted, and focused to such a bright point that it became a physical menace. For six minutes the upper level was paralyzed; the cash registers were cocooned behind the moaning, kneeling bodies pressed together; customers were trapped; business could not be done. The terror-stricken personnel tried in vain to force the crowd out. "Is anyone making a purchase?" one was heard to call out weakly. As the mob dispersed down the escalators and out into the street, the police were downstairs, telling us to leave, but we had already accomplished the task, had delivered what was in effect a warning.

Almost unanimously, though, the bloggers panned MOB #6. "Another Mob Botched" was the verdict on the blog Fancy Robot: "[I]nstead of setting the Flash Mob out in public on Times Square itself, as everyone had hoped, The Flash Master decided to set it in Toys 'R' Us, with apparently dismal results." SatansLaundromat.com (a photo-blog that contains the most complete visual record of the New York project) concurred—"not public enough," the blogger wrote, without enough "spectators to bewilder"—as did Chris from the CCE Blog: "I think the common feeling among these blogger reviews is: where does the idea go from here? . . . After seeing hundreds of people show up for no good reason, it's obvious that there's some kind of potential for artistic or political expression here."

The idea seemed to be that flash mobs could be made to convey a message, but for a number of reasons this dream was destined to run aground. First, as outlined above, flash mobs were gatherings of *insiders,* and as such could hardly communicate to those who did not already belong. They were intramural play; they drew their energies not from impressing outsiders or freaking them out but from showing them utter disregard, from using the outside world as merely a terrain for private games. Second, in terms of time, flash mobs were by definition *transitory,* ten minutes or fewer, and thereby not exactly suited to standing their ground and testifying. Third, in terms of physical space, flash mobs relied on *constraints* to create an illusion of superior strength. I never held mobs in the open, the bloggers complained, in view of enough onlookers, but this was entirely purposeful on my part, for like Colin Powell I hewed to a doctrine of overwhelming force. Only in enclosed spaces could the mob generate the necessary self-awe; to allow the mob to feel small would have been to destroy it.

The following week, the interview request from the *New York Times* finally arrived. On the phone the reporter, Amy Harmon, made it clear to me that the *Times* knew it was behind on the story. The paper would be remedying this, she told me, by running a prominent piece on flash mobs in its Sunday Week in Review section. What the *Times* did, in fascinating fashion, was not just to run the backlash story (which I had been expecting in three to five more weeks) but to do so preemptively— i.e., before there was actually a backlash. Harmon's piece bore the headline GUESS SOME PEOPLE DON'T HAVE ANYTHING BETTER TO DO, and its nut sentence ran: "[T]he flash mob juggernaut has now run into a flash mob backlash that may be spreading faster than the fad itself." As evidence, she mustered the following:

> E-mail lists like "antimob" and "slashmob" have sprung up, as did a Web site warning that "flashmuggers" are bound to show up "wherever there's groups of young, naïve, wealthy, bored fashionistas to be found." And a new definition was circulated last week on several Web sites: "flash mob, noun: An impromptu

gathering, organized by means of electronic communication, of the unemployed."

Two e-mail lists, a website, and a forwarded definition hardly constituted a "backlash" against this still-growing, intercontinental fad, but what I think Harmon and the *Times* rightly understood was that a backlash was the only avenue by which they could advance the story, i.e., find a new narrative. Whether through direct causation or mere journalistic intuition, the *Times* timed its backlash story (8/17/03) with remarkable accuracy:

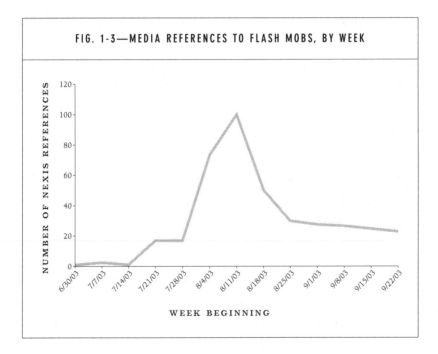

FIG. 1-3—MEDIA REFERENCES TO FLASH MOBS, BY WEEK

PERMUTATIONS

Whether the backlash was real or not, it almost didn't matter: there was no way for the flash mob to keep growing, and since the entire logic of the mob was to grow, the mob was destined to die. It couldn't become political, or even make any statement at all, within the prescribed confines of a ten-minute burst. After six mobs, even conceiving of new enough crowd permutations started to feel like a challenge. We had done consumers collaborating (MOB #2) and consumers not collaborating (MOB #4). We had done an ecstatic, moaning throng (MOB #6) and a more sedate, absurdist one (MOB #5, in which the mob hid in some Central Park woods and simulated animal noises). In MOB #3, we had formed an inward-facing ring, and the idea of another geometrical mob appealed to me. I decided that MOB #7, set for late August, should be a queue.

Scouting locations had become in many ways the most pleasant task of the experiment. Roughly a week before each appointed day, having chosen the neighborhood in advance, I would stroll nonchalantly around the streets, looking at parks and stairways and stores, imagining a few hundred people descending at once upon each: How would such a mob arrive? How would it array itself? What would it do? Could it be beautiful? For MOB #7 I had picked Midtown, the commercial heart of the city, and so one Thursday in the late afternoon I took the subway uptown from my office to envision a crowd. I started on Fiftieth Street at Eighth Avenue and walked east, slipping through the milling Broadway tourists: too much real crowd for a fake crowd to stand out successfully. At Sixth Avenue I eyed Radio City Music Hall—an inviting target, to be sure, but the sidewalk in front was too narrow, too trafficked, for a mob comfortably to do its work. At Rockefeller Center, I eyed the Christmas tree spot, which was empty that August; but there was far too much security lurking about.

When I arrived at Fifth Avenue, though, and looked up at the spires of Saint Patrick's Cathedral, I realized I had found just the place. A paramount Manhattan landmark with not much milling out front (since tourists were generally allowed inside); a sacred site, moreover, all the better for profaning with a disposable crowd. Crossing Fifth, I started around the structure from the north, following it to Madison and coming around the south side back to Fifth Avenue. I wanted a line, but it would be too risky to have it start at the front doors, since the cathedral staff that stood near the door might disperse it before it could fully form. But on each side of the cathedral, I noticed, was a small wooden door, not open to the public. If a line began at one of these doors, it could wind around the grand structure but keep staff confused long enough to last for the allotted five minutes. I stood at the corner of Fiftieth and Fifth, pondering what should happen after that. Flash mobbers were mostly people like me, downtown and Brooklyn kids, a demographic seldom seen in either Midtown or church. I loved the idea that Saint Patrick's might somehow have inexplicably become cool, a place where if one lined up at the side door, one might stand a chance of getting in for—*what?* Tickets to see some stupidly cool band, I thought; and in the summer of 2003 the right band to make fun of was the Strokes, a band had been clearly manufactured, Monkees-like, precisely for our delectation. It was settled, then: the mob would line up from the small door on the north side, wind around the front and down the south side. When passersby asked why they were lining up, mobbers were to say they "heard they're selling Strokes tickets."

Having settled the script that Thursday afternoon, I started back down Fiftieth, only to see a man walk out of the side door. He was a short man with curly hair tight to his head, and he wore a knit blue tie over a white patterned button-down shirt. Without acknowledging me in any way, he walked to the curb and then stood still, staring up at the sky. Back at Madison, I saw that since I last was at the corner, the stoplight had gone dark: an uncommon city sight. As I headed south down Madison, weaving through accumulating traffic crowding crosswalks, more people began to trickle out of the office buildings, looking dazed, rubbing their eyes in the sunlight. A woman dressed as Nefertiti was fanning herself. Customers lined up at bodegas to buy bottles of water. I thought I would walk south until I got out of the blackout zone; by

Union Square I realized that the blackout zone was very large indeed, though it was not until I got back to work, walking the eleven flights up, that I was told the zone was not just all of New York City but most of the northeastern United States. Having spent my last half hour envisioning my own absurdist mob, I had suddenly stepped into a citywide flash mob planned by no one, born not of a will to metaspectacle but of basic human need. The power returned within the week, and MOB #7 went on exactly as planned; but to gather a crowd on New York's streets never felt quite the same, and I knew my days making mobs were dwindling fast.

DOWN: BOREDOM REDUX

I wrote of boredom as inspiring the mob's birth; but I suspect that boredom helped to hasten its death, as well—the boredom, that is, of the constantly distracted mind. This paradoxical relationship between boredom and distraction was demonstrated elegantly in 1989, by psychologists at Clark University in Worcester, Massachusetts. Ninety-one undergraduates, broken up into small groups, were played a tape-recorded reading of fifteen minutes in length, but during the playback for some of the students a modest distraction was introduced: the sound of a TV soap opera, playing at a "just noticeable" level. Afterward, when the students were asked if their minds had wandered during the recording, the results were as to be expected. Seventy percent of the intentionally distracted listeners said their minds had wandered, as opposed to 55 percent of the control group. What was far more surprising, however, were the reasons they gave: among those whose minds wandered, 76 percent of the distracted listeners said this was because the tape was "boring," versus only 41 percent of their non-distracted counterparts. We tend to think of boredom as a response to having too few external stimuli, but here boredom was perceived more keenly at the precise time that more stimuli were present.

The experiment's authors, Robin Damrad-Frye and James Laird, argue that the results make sense in the context of "self-perception theory": the notion that we determine our internal states in large part by observing our own behavior. Other studies have supported this general idea. Subjects asked to mimic a certain emotion will then report feeling that emotion. Subjects made to argue in favor of a statement, either through a speech or an essay, will afterward attest to believing it. Subjects forced to gaze into each other's eyes will later profess sexual attraction for each other. In the case of boredom, the authors write, "The reason people know they are bored is, at least in part, that they find they cannot keep their attention focused where it should be." That is, they ascribe their own inattention to a deficiency not in themselves, or in their surroundings, but in that to which they are supposed to be attending.

Today, in the advanced stages of our information age, with our e-mail in-boxes and phones and instant messages all chirping for our attention, it is as if we are conducting Damrad-Frye and Laird's experiment on a society-wide scale. Gloria Mark, a professor at the University of California at Irvine, has found that white-collar officeworkers can work for only eleven minutes, on average, without being interrupted. Among the young, permanent distraction is a way of life: the majority of seventh- to twelfth-graders in the United States say that they "multitask"—using other media—some or even most of the time they are reading or using the computer. The writer and software expert Linda Stone has called this lifestyle one of "continuous partial attention," an elegant phrase to describe the endless wave of electronic distraction that so many of us ride. There is ample evidence that all this distraction impairs our ability to do things well: a psychologist at the University of Michigan found that multitasking subjects made more errors in each task and took from 50 to 100 percent more time to finish. But far more intriguing, I think, is how our constant distraction may be feeding back into our perception of the world—the effect observed among those Clark undergraduates, writ large; the sense, that is, that nothing we attend to is adequate, precisely because nothing can escape the roiling scorn of our distraction.

This, finally, is what kills nanostories, I think, and what surely killed the flash mob, not only in the media but in my own mind: this always-encroaching boredom, this need to tell ever *new stories* about our society and ourselves, even when there are no new stories to be told. This impulse itself is far from new, of course; it is a species of what Neil Postman meant in 1984 when he decried the culture of news as entertainment, and indeed of what Daniel Boorstin meant in 1961 when he railed against our "extravagant expectations" for the world of human events. What viral culture adds is, in part, just pure acceleration—the speed born of more data sources, more frequent updates, more churn—but far more crucially it adds interactivity, and with it a perverse kind of market democracy. As more of us take on the media mantle ourselves, telling our own stories rather than allowing others to tell them for us, it is we who can act to assuage our own boredom, our inadequacy, our despair by projecting them out through how we describe the world.

DISPERSAL

I announced that MOB #8, in early September, would be the last. The invitation e-mail's subject was *MOB #8: The end,* and the text began with a FAQ:

Q. The end?

A. Yes.

Q. Why?

A. It can't be explained. Like the individual mobs, the Mob Project appeared for no reason, and like the mobs it must disperse.

Q. Will the Mob Project ever reappear?

A. It might. But don't expect it.

The site was a concrete alcove right on Forty-second Street, just across from the Condé Nast building. Participants had been told to follow the instructions blaring from a cheap boom box I had set up beforehand atop a brick ledge. I had prerecorded a tape of myself, barking out commands. I envisioned my hundreds of mobbers, following the dictates of what was effectively a loudspeaker on a pole. It was hard to get more straightforward than that, I thought.

But the cheering of the hundreds grew so great that it drowned out the speakers. The mob soon became unmoored. All of a sudden a man in a toque, apparently some sort of opportunistic art shaman, opened his briefcase to reveal a glowing neon sign, and the crowd bent to his will. He held up two fingers, and to my horror the mob began chanting "Peace!" In retrospect, I saw it as a fitting end for an experiment about bandwagons and conformity, about inattention and media hype. My crowd had ultimately been hijacked by a figure more mysterious, more enigmatic than even the semianonymous "Bill"—by a better story, that is, than me.

Of all my experiments in viral culture, the Mob Project was by far the most impressive in its spread; and indeed this spread spurred much of my ensuing interest in the subject. In starting the project, my major interest had been in the intersection of the virtual and the physical—I had seen the mob as a way for online connections to manifest themselves visually, corporeally, disruptively in the sidewalks and spaces of urban life. But as the mob grew beyond my most optimistic projections, and then collapsed, I became less fixated on the mobs themselves and more focused on the *storytelling* about them. The arc of a mob, of the Mob Project, of flash mobs as a general phenomenon, of the media narrative *about* the phenomenon—all were strangely congruent in the rapid rise and fall, and I desperately wanted to understand the story-telling that made these spikes operate.

Chapter 2 is an exploration of the most basic breeding ground for spikes, and the stories—i.e., the nanostories—that fuel them: the *niche*, or *subculture*, which the Internet as a medium has both invigorated and transformed.

2.

ANNUALS

EXPERIMENT: STOP PETER
BJORN AND JOHN

SUBCULTURES OF NARCISSISM

In June 2004 a twenty-nine-year-old prosecutor named David Lat, who spent his days working at the U.S. Attorney's Office in Newark, New Jersey, began a hobby that eventually elevated him as an icon of both his profession and his time. Adopting a persona called "Article III Groupie," a drink-addled female devotee of constitutional law, he began writing a legal blog—Underneath Their Robes—which promised, in its first post and de facto manifesto, to apply the methodology of celebrity magazines (Lat listed as his models *People, Us Weekly, Page Six, The National Enquirer,* and *Tiger Beat*) to the rarefied culture of appeals-court juristry. In an early series of posts, Lat selected the "Superhotties of the Federal Judiciary," male and female; of Supreme Court justice David Souter he wrote, "Certiorari is GRANTED to that hot, lean body!" Lat encouraged readers to send in anonymously sourced "blind items" on high-ranking judges, whose identities would be left to the reader's best guess, e.g.:

> This southeastern district judge had her clerks pack her belongings
> so she could move out after she and her husband filed for divorce.

> This well-known circuit court judge . . . has issues concerning
> the appropriate treatment of female clerks in his chambers.

The dark joke underlying Lat's antics was obvious: take the lowest form of cultural analysis (celebrity gossip), apply it to one of the more intellectual and obscure reaches of American life (appellate law), and what you get is comedy gold. Except it didn't play as comedy, or at least not *just* as comedy. Appellate judges really *were* a sort of celebrity to a certain—if small—segment of the population, namely those lawyers who, like Lat, worked in that corner of the profession. These lawyers all avidly read Lat's blog. Few of them had previously thought of their profession as a hotbed of salacious gossip, but once a site had bothered to collect it all and present it in a jaundiced tone, the evidence was indisputable. During the two years that Lat kept up his blog (before he was exposed and stepped down from his day job), Underneath Their Robes not only tweaked its profession but on some level transformed it. The lofty reaches of constitutional law had become infected with the media mind.

So it has gone with other subcultures in our viral age, when the Internet—with its worldwide accessibility and infinite capacity for segmentation—has allowed us to connect with farther-flung people who are more and more like ourselves. Much of the emergent Internet culture is in fact a collection of a wide array of *niche* cultures, in keeping with the "Long Tail" argument put forward by *Wired* editor Chris Anderson in his book of that name: "People are re-forming," he writes, "into thousands of cultural *tribes of interest,* connected less by geographic proximity and workplace chatter than by shared interests." But what the Internet has done is arguably less to form such tribes than to change how they see themselves. Think about the offline publications that have traditionally catered to subcultures: many of them can still be found lining the magazine racks of one's local Barnes & Noble, those rows of sleepy titles devoted to individual professions, sports teams, musical genres, political preferences, ethnic communities, and so on. The very way we find these publications, each tucked among a slew of unrelated others, makes us keenly aware of their narrow purview, and one can sense in their pages that they realize this too. The difference online, where subcultures converse incessantly among themselves in an intense, always-on, inwardly directed banter, is that every crowd comes to talk and think about itself as if it were the center of the entire universe.

The most obvious symptom of this shift has been the online democratization of fame—what the technology writer Clive Thompson has dubbed "microcelebrity." Just as David Lat treated the 877 members of the appellate judiciary (and sometimes even their clerks!) as celebrities, and just as some flash-mobbers wanted to make "Bill" into a movement luminary, so does each subculture online tend to coronate its own small claque of mini-stars. On the Silicon Valley gossip blog Valleywag, readers follow the exploits of the young founders of Google and Facebook (and of far lesser business figures such as Jakob Lodwick, a marginally successful young web entrepreneur whose chief occupation seems to be seeking microcelebrity) in the same manner that *Us Weekly* stalks Tom Cruise. Even within user-run communities, fame finds a way of attaching itself to the most provocative members. The *New York Times* reported that when "DaShiv"—a photographer and popular commenter on the group blog MetaFilter—came to visit New York, three different parties were given in his honor by online associates.

But such nanofame is just part of a larger move toward nanostories— toward more narratives, and more perishable narratives—that has taken place within online subcultures. The reason for this larger shift is simple: the blinding speed and vast capacity of the medium essentially requires it. If impassioned chatter keeps up for days over the question of whether the forthcoming Corvette engine was unduly copied from a

BMW engine—as was the case in early January 2008 on Autoblog, the biggest blog for car enthusiasts—it is only because a community that reviews twenty or more "breaking" car news stories in any given day will naturally seize on at least one story a week as earth-shattering. Moreover, the writers, seeing how readers love squabbles, begin to bake this into their posts: one imagines that PurseBlog, a site that reviews designer handbags, would not get two hundred thousand visits a day (making it by one count the twentieth-most popular blog in America) if it did not regularly trash high-priced bags as "fug." (In one case, about a bag that went "out on a limb," it remarked: "Your limb is hanging over a river infested with piranhas and your branch just broke.") In the past, niche cultures were less fickle than the mainstream, because their adherents, aware of their marginal status and prizing group loyalty, wanted nothing more than to trumpet their own stars and stories into the wider culture. But today, when each subculture gets more niche news than even its fanatics can swallow, members become starved for deeper diversions, and their hit-hungry sites are more than happy to oblige.

Not long ago, I spent six months following the niche culture of indie rock—the loose musical genre, popular among collegians and young urbanites, that is defined not by any particular sound but by an opposition to (or at least exclusion from) corporate radio and labels. This subculture predates the Internet, to be sure; its lineage stretches back to the hardcore scene of the 1980s, if not before, and as a community it has been perpetuated through the years by a network of college radio stations, rundown clubs, obscure magazines, and boutique record stores. Precisely because of its oppositional roots, indie rock (like punk before it) had an even more fierce devotion than other niches to its subcultural stars: acts like Fugazi, the Pixies, Guided by Voices. But the Internet has utterly transformed indie rock, as tracks leaked through MySpace and file-sharing have allowed unknown bands to become overnight subcultural sensations, their uptake and abandonment egged on by scores of popular blogs. After observing some of these spikes flicker through the hipster hive-mind, I wondered whether I might choose one and attempt, as best I could, to document it as it actually happened. What I found, in the story of a band called Annuals, was a parable not just of fickle indie-rock fame but of a paradoxical new cultural force: the rise of niche sensationalism.

GET READY TO GET SICK

On July 17, 2006, a man named Mike on the indie-rock blog Postcore .com made what could only be called a preemptive strike. "[W]ord on the street," he wrote, "is that Pitchfork"—the Internet's most influential music site, and arguably the independent music scene's chief tastemaker, online or off—"is getting the jump on this band tomorrow, which means we're going to throw it out there today." He went on:

> [T]his band's got it all: young songwriter who begs for the "wunderkind" title . . . inventive and semi-electronic production, full support from the most influential music blog out there (not this one), songs that explode halfway through, and about a hundred music blogs who feel the pressure to write about a different band every day. I'm just saying, get ready to get sick of hearing about this band.

"Get ready to get sick of hearing about this band": it would be difficult to think of a more apt motto for indie rock—or any niche culture, for that matter—in the age of the Internet. Finding out about important new culture used to depend on whom you knew or where you were. In the indie-rock scene of the 1980s, news spread almost exclusively through word of mouth, through photocopied 'zines (often with circulations in three or even two digits), or through low-watt college radio stations. Today, indie-rock culture remains an underground culture, basically by definition, in that its fans shun mainstream music in favor of lesser-known acts. But now, MySpace, iTunes, and Internet radio make location and friends irrelevant for discovering music. Blogs and aggregators enable fans to determine in just a few minutes what everyone else is listening to that day. What you know, where you are—these matter not at all. To be an insider today one must merely be *fast*. Once Mike found out that Pitchfork would be posting about the new band, one cannot blame him for his haste, because *après* Pitchfork *le déluge:* unknown bands become all-too-familiar bands in a month, and abandoned bands the month after that. Get ready, that is, to get sick.

As promised, half past ten on the morning of July 18 saw Ryan Schreiber, the founder and editor in chief of Pitchfork, place his imprimatur upon the new band, which he likened to "some fantasy hybrid of Animal Collective, Arcade Fire, and Broken Social Scene." His readers would know these names—bands that ranked among the most successful indie-rock acts of the previous four years, all of which (not coincidentally) owed a debt to Pitchfork in getting there. Schreiber had essentially launched Broken Social Scene's career when he described their American debut album—which he said in his review that he had found just by "dig[ging] through the boxes upon boxes of promos that arrive at the Pitchfork mailbox each month"—as "endlessly replayable, perfect pop." More recently, a Schreiber review had conferred indie-rock superstardom on Brooklyn's Clap Your Hands Say Yeah, which did not even have a record deal (the band had self-produced its album). What makes Pitchfork so powerful is not the size of its readership, which by web-magazine standards is small: one and a half million visitors each month, only a fraction of whom read the site regularly. Rather, it is its stature in the firmament of indie-rock blogs as a kind of North Star, a point of reference to be measured against. A glowing Pitchfork review need not be agreed with, but it must at the very least be reckoned with. In his post about the new band, Schreiber concluded with a wink to his site's clout. "Get familiar now," he wrote, "we could be writing about these dudes all year long." Predictably, by the end of August, more than thirty blogs had posted about the new band, and the album's leaked tracks became fixtures on the Hot Tracks list at Elbo.ws, a site that monitors plays of downloaded music.

Once Pitchfork blesses an act, any mention of that act on other blogs needs to be accompanied by an acknowledgment that one has lagged terribly behind the times. On September 7, Stereogum.com not only quoted Pitchfork's review but wrote, "The hype machine"—by which they presumably meant blogs like themselves, because not a single dollar had yet gone into promoting the new band—"has been in motion for this band, so we feel sorta silly calling them a Band to Watch (we know, we know . . . *you* blogged about them first)." Even so, the first comment, just fifteen minutes after the post, began with one word in all caps: "DUH." By September 18, Idolator, the music blog of Gawker Media's online empire, could pull back for a world-weary dissection of the new band as phenomenon, complete with "Odds of Backlash," which it placed at 5:1. On October 5, when *Rolling Stone* magazine's "Rock and Roll Daily" blog finally weighed in, with an unctuous pronouncement of phony hipness—"Trust us on this one: you guys are gonna seriously sweat us for introducing you" to this band—commenter "nick" unloaded with justifiably righteous scorn:

> yeah . . . everyone is really gonna "sweat you" for being (LITER-ALLY) the last blog on the Internet to write baout these guys.

The band was called Annuals, and they hailed from Raleigh, North Carolina. I first heard the tracks on October 14, three days before their official release but three months too late. Their sound is difficult to describe, especially to those who have not heard Animal Collective, Arcade Fire, or Broken Social Scene, bands that plumbed the sonic expansiveness afforded by our high-tech, DIY musical age, when one can emerge from one's basement with music that is meticulously untidy, offhandedly epic. And if these other bands were epic, Annuals were more so. Within a single song, the vocal might rise from tender contemplation to a wail or even a hoarse, toneless scream; drums, hitherto absent, suddenly charge in, mammoth, driving, relentless, with two or even three kits going at once; arpeggios from various synths and strings wander in and out while electronica decorates the margins, a layered sheet of rigorous noise. What Annuals will sound like to you today I cannot say, but in the autumn of 2006, they sounded like the future.

GET A DYNASTY TOGETHER

Two weeks later I met Annuals in New York, at a vegan grocery/café on the Lower East Side. They had come to the city for the CMJ Music Marathon, a sort of indie-rock hajj for hundreds of bands, some of whom play to capacity crowds while others, bleeding flagellants, must play to almost no one—as I learned firsthand earlier in the week when, at the 7:00 p.m. set of a band I had liked online (a wistful, countrified act called The Western States Motel), I found myself in an audience of perhaps a half dozen, a situation in which one finds rock bands starting to make discomforting levels of eye contact. But already it had been guaranteed that Annuals would draw a crowd. Although the band's time slot was poor—number two on a six-band bill—their success at the festival had been essentially preordained, as everyone had seen the online blowup and modified their expectations accordingly. Even the *New York Times*, the day I met the band, had fingered Annuals, with their "grand, disheveled songs," as the festival band most likely to make good.

The orchestrator of Annuals was Adam Baker, a scruffy but strikingly purposive twenty-year-old. A meld of hipster and hippie, he wore a green hoodie, rolled-up cords, and junked-out white Asics but also kept a little ponytail and a thin, messy beard, and wore a blue satin cord as a choker. He spoke in a businesslike patter, his eyes darting around, a young man residing very much inside his own capacious head. With his mouth full of some sort of health food, he talked to me about creative control and how he aimed to maintain it. "That's been, like, our only rider throughout this whole thing," he said. "You can't force us to do it any other way than how we know how. We had tried recording with producers from the start, doing all the tracking with someone else and having them at the board? But it really makes us uncomfortable, and the sound doesn't come out exactly how we want it."

Instead, Adam recorded and produced all the songs essentially by himself. If he owed his band's sudden popularity to the Internet, he owed his creative control to an equally revolutionary technology: PC-based sound-engineering software, particularly Pro Tools, which has become cheap (a stripped-down version is free), remarkably powerful, and now basically ubiquitous; Adam is of a generation of musicians accustomed to producing CD-quality music in their teenage bedrooms. He had wrecked one of his eardrums, but unlike rockers of yore he incurred his injury not with amps on a stage but with headphones plugged into a computer.

Lead guitar in Annuals was handled by Kenny Florence, a gregarious, almost antic nineteen-year-old with a baby face and thick black hair closely cropped. The six members of Annuals also played together as a band called Sedona, a sort of indie-bluegrass affair led by Kenny with Adam on drums. In fact, it was while on tour as Sedona, in the van, that they got the call from a record label that had discovered Adam's Annuals songs on MySpace. Now Sedona lingered in the background while Annuals got its turn. "Annuals is our main project right now," Kenny said, "but we plan on putting out lots of different albums with lots of different styles and lots of different ideas. . . . We're planning on pretty much just like—I don't know what the word is—*exploding* people's brains with all of the projects that we're doing, you know?"

"The intention is to get a dynasty together, I guess," added Adam. They spoke in the half-ironic tone affected today when expressing great dreams. In the meantime, Kenny still lived with his parents, while Adam roomed with bassist Mike Robinson. "In my mom's basement," interjected Mike. "Can't lie."

"Can't afford a fucking apartment, man," said Adam.

"We're still climbing the hill," Mike said philosophically.

Kenny, Adam, and Mike had been playing together since their early teens, when they had a punk band called Timothy's Weekend. That was in 2000, they said—*2000!*—and suddenly the youth of these guys struck me. They played with the sophisticated sound of bands five or ten years older.

"We've been probably playing music together for the same amount of time they've been playing," Kenny pointed out.

"We just got a head start, that's all," offered Adam. He added that they hadn't even listened to Arcade Fire, Animal Collective, or Broken Social Scene until the comparisons started. His own influences, he said, tended toward the older: Paul Simon, Brian Wilson. "They're just trying to compare us to bands that are current, you know?" he said. "There's not really anyone else they *can* compare us to." He paused. "I *think*."

THE HIPSTER CONSENSUS

In *The Long Tail*, Chris Anderson saw the Internet as taking us out of a "watercooler" era—when we "listened, watched, and read from the same, relatively small pool of mostly hit content"—into the "microculture" era, when "we're all into different things." Anderson's conclusion on this score is predicated on the basic economist's view of human nature: we each have preexisting tastes and preferences, and we use our market choices to satisfy them as best we can. As a medium, the Internet is indeed unprecedented in its ability to sustain fan bases around anything, and thereby segment us around narrow interests. But as we saw in chapter 1, the Internet is also an unprecedented medium for the bandwagon effect, which sways large numbers of people not through some atomized personal choices of each but through each being influenced by the herd behavior of the rest.

The phenomenon that Anderson described is certainly happening, for much the same reasons that our profusion of cable-TV channels has made it impossible for any show, even the Super Bowl, to garner the overwhelming market share that could be achieved in the days of only three networks. More choice translates into more fragmentation. But I would argue that the Internet is working in two contradictory ways on the cultural landscape, and that the interaction between the two forces—the "Long Tail" effect (toward ever splintering niches) and the bandwagon effect (toward more clustering around the same thing)—is a complicated and intriguing one. Think about just this wrinkle: through the Internet, our microcultures all now have watercoolers of their own, and the social pressure *within* those cultures to rally around common cultural products can be far greater than in the old, offline world. Also: our microcultures, being available online to membership by everyone at all times, can become magnets for huge followings—at which point, arguably, they are not so "micro" anymore.

This has certainly become the case with indie rock, which is more broadly popular by far than it was during the hardcore or college-rock days, and perhaps even more popular than during the corporate-marketed "alternative" rock heyday of the early 1990s. It has become the musical lingua franca of an entire demographic of not just college students but a large chunk of educated urban twenty- and thirtysome-things, whether in New York or San Francisco or D.C. or Seattle. They all vote Democrat, too, and in this regard they reside in the "urban archipelago," as a very smart essay in Seattle alt-weekly *The Stranger* called the urban liberal consensus just after the heartbreaking (for us) 2004 election. But more remarkable than this nationwide political consensus is the nationwide cultural consensus that has sprung up within or alongside it. Far from splintering into ever narrower niches, this cultural consensus has extended its reach through the Internet, constituting a sort of universal urban middlebrow.

One might call this the "hipster" consensus, to use the somewhat unfortunate term that (for better or for worse) has come to denote these educated young Americans; and no cultural genre defines this consensus more than does indie rock. And if this hipster archipelago is a virtual community, it is building up its own virtual institutions, which use the Internet to harmonize the far-flung members, to allow these thousands of disparate agents to maintain a near-instantaneous and deceptively easy unanimity. Pitchfork serves as one of these institutions, as does the Gawker Media network of blogs (which includes the aforementioned Idolator, as well as Gawker in New York, Defamer in L.A., and a handful of other, nongeographically aligned offerings). But perhaps more intriguing than either of these is KEXP, a real-world public-radio station in Seattle that attracts a significant portion of its listenership online. Its three prime-time DJs play almost entirely indie rock, with selections that (broadly) mirror the lineups, themselves converging, of the nation's indie-rock clubs. And indeed, a list of KEXP's top-twelve cities for online listenership reads like a hipster-archipelago roll call (albeit weighted understandably westward):

FIG. 2-1: KEXP STREAMING CITIES

RANK	CITY	PERCENT
1	Seattle	24.17%
2	New York	14.38%
3	Minneapolis	8.28%
4	Portland, Ore.	6.92%
5	Chicago	5.99%
6	San Francisco	5.26%
7	Los Angeles	3.43%
8	Washington, D.C.	3.35%
9	Vancouver	2.80%
10	Denver	2.78%
11	Atlanta	2.69%
12	Austin, Tex.	2.13%

(Numbers 13 and 15, curiously enough, are Beijing and Guangzhou, in China.) Although it should be stressed that the actual online tribe of KEXP, like that of Pitchfork, is relatively small—62,000 unique visitors per week—it nevertheless functions as a crucial pollinator of sounds, injecting the same new bands at the exact same time into similar social groups around the world.

The week I met Annuals, during the CMJ festival in New York, KEXP played host to a series of studio appearances by what one could only call, without any cynicism, some of the new bands of the season— Bound Stems, Hot Chip, White Whale, Forward Russia, Tokyo Police Club, What Made Milwaukee Famous—as well as appearances from such admired older bands as the Shins and the Apples in Stereo. (Annuals had already recorded at the station in Seattle, a few weeks beforehand.) The day I visited, the show featured a Norwegian electronic band called 120 Days. In a blond-wood-paneled anteroom, the audience sat on folding chairs while behind the studio window the band gamely tried, as synth acts must, to give off the appearance of "rocking" while they attended to their machines. All of them strained to lurch about kinetically as they tweaked the knobs on their Korgs.

Midway through this arid demonstration, I retreated to sit down with John Richards, KEXP's morning-show host and probably the most listened-to indie-rock DJ in the nation. Richards has a slight build, an elfin face, and dirty-blond hair parted down the middle. Now in his mid-thirties, he had started as an intern at the station (under its previous name, KCMU) and worked his way all the way up to drivetime. His taste is bulletproof; I find myself constantly checking the real-time playlist during his online broadcasts to catch the names of the bands. When I asked him about the "virtual community" of indie rock, he knew just what I was talking about. He brought up the band Tapes 'n Tapes, a breakout act of spring 2006 (Pitchfork review: 8.3 out of 10) that perversely had not even attracted much of an audience in its own hometown of Minneapolis until it was picked up by the various blogs and by KEXP.

"A listener in Austin told me about it," Richards recalled. "I sent somebody off to find the music—'Find this right away,' I said. . . . We got the demo from the band within a week, and started playing it." The trick in breaking bands, Richards said, is repetition. "Cowbell"—Tapes 'n Tapes' first hit, a driving raw thing—"was the song I was hitting constantly. And just kept hitting it, and hitting it, and hitting it, and then all of a sudden you saw their hometown suddenly react to a station playing their band. And then it just grew from there."

It was a great story, Tapes 'n Tapes, every bit as good as the story of Annuals. A new band, sprung up from nothing to become something— this was the prototypical tale told by music journalists, of which I happened to be one. As Richards poured out his enthusiasm, as we sat there on a beat-up leather couch, 120 Days was still next door, plying their synths in the studio: another new band and another great story, no doubt. But a question nagged at me, and I put it to Richards with almost a twinge of embarrassment, at asking him to interrupt his reverie about new bands. Why did so many of these bands disappear? What about the second album, or the third? Why did indie rock seem to have become wave after wave of disposable new bands? Richards thought for a bit before answering.

"You have these bands working really, really hard," he replied. "They're writing great songs, they've had five years maybe; and their best material is going to make it on their first album." But then, he went on, "You have a label involved at this point, you have deadlines now— another album in six months, nine months."

Richards said he now assumed that he would not even see second albums, even from bands he loved, no matter how good their sound. "Even an Annuals," he said. "I'm not even thinking about a second album from them. I just assume that this is the document that I have. . . . You think: 'This is a great movie—I hope there's not a sequel.'"

But when pressed further, Richards acknowledged that he and the other indie-rock tastemakers bore some share of the blame. "A big deal with us is discovery," he said. "And you're discovering not just a song; you're discovering a *band*. When you're just discovering a second album, there's not as much hype involved." He began to recount his own discovery of the Pixies, in 1988, and as he spoke his speech became subtly emotional, his hands began to clench. "I heard *Surfer Rosa* when I walked in a record store, and it changed my life. And you know, all the other albums I heard after that were great, but man, it never equaled that.... It was like a drug, I guess. You take the drug, you never get that high again, you know?"

He laughed at this, but he was coming to the crux of something. "It gets harder and harder to achieve that," he said. "You keep thinking— I want to be the one to discover that band. When you hear someone talk about Clap Your Hands Say Yeah, and you're hearing that David Byrne loves them, or David Bowie. And—wow, I saw them! And it was packed!

"But the second time," he went on, "well, now it sold out early, and it's at a bigger club. And *I'm not that guy anymore. I'm not the guy discovering them.* I'm just a guy who is with everybody else who also knows who they are."

THERE'S TWO SIDES TO THAT SHIT

One unlikely outpost of the hipster archipelago can be found in a strip mall in Carrboro, North Carolina. At the rightmost end of a startlingly hideous facade, the top half of which consists of some strange, brown corrugated metal that harkens back to 1980s slapdash futurism, the Cat's Cradle sits nonchalantly, as if a rock club somehow naturally belonged there alongside the video store and the Amante Gourmet Pizza. Despite its prosaic setting, the club is a longstanding and vital node in the national indie-rock network. To scan the list of bands playing at Cat's Cradle in any given year is to get a decent sense for the "big" indie bands that are touring the United States that year; one would find general overlap with any list of bands playing at, for example, the Bowery Ballroom or the Knitting Factory in New York; at the 9:30 Club or the Black Cat in Washington, D.C.; at First Avenue or the 400 Bar in Minneapolis; at the Middle East in Boston; at Hailey's in Denton, Texas; at the Casbah in San Diego; at the Earl in Atlanta; at the Metro or the Abbey in Chicago; at Bimbo's or the Independent in San Francisco; at Chop Suey or the Showbox in Seattle; or at the shows put on in Philadelphia by Sean Agnew's R5 Productions, many of which take place in the basement of a Unitarian church—an even odder spot, perhaps, for indie-rock shows than a strip mall.

In January, three months after I first met Annuals in New York, I came to see them in their hometown, or roughly so: it was at the Cat's Cradle and the other clubs in Carrboro—and Chapel Hill, home to UNC, which Carrboro abuts—that all of them got their start playing music. While the band waited to do their soundcheck, we sat around in the green room, which looked much like green rooms in seedy rock clubs anywhere: a dorm-room fridge, haphazardly arrayed scraps of torn carpet, fourth-hand upholstered furniture with springs distended out the undersides.

"Whose Pop-Tarts are these?" asked Anna Spence, the slender redhead who played keyboards in the band.

"Mine," said Kenny.

"*Ours,*" said Adam, whose preshow preparations consisted of pacing around while using a lighter to burn decorative holes in his white collared shirt. "That's our rider, baby! Pop-Tarts."

By indie-rock standards, the past three months had been extraordinarily good to Annuals: an appearance on *Late Night with Conan O'Brien*, a full-page article in *Rolling Stone*. But they were still, as Mike had put it, "climbing the hill," and the band's patience with touring seemed to be fraying somewhat. "There's a plan to take a big break," Adam said, "because we've got all these other projects." He was speaking chiefly of

Sedona, in which he drummed—"I'm *dying* to get back behind the set," he said. But he rattled off two other side projects as well: bassist Mike had a "folk-pop" act called First Person Plural, plus Adam was planning an electronica act that he said was called Tundra.

Annuals was coming through their hometown with almost no fan-fare, playing as the opener for the Dears—an unfortunately maudlin rock act from Montreal whose songs, as a friend aptly put it later during the show, resembled nothing so much as "a musical about an indie-rock band." I couldn't help but think about how the whole notion of a homegrown scene, here as elsewhere, had disappeared. Fifteen years ago, to be sure, national bands came through the Chapel Hill–area clubs, but it also meant something to speak of a Chapel Hill band, and a Chapel Hill sound; the lo-fi pop sensibility of Superchunk, Archers of Loaf, and Polvo defined a local identity. Today in Chapel Hill, former members of Superchunk run Merge Records—arguably the nation's most influential indie label—but its bands hail from around the United States, Canada, and even Europe. Annuals, whose label was run until recently out of a cramped one-bedroom apartment on Fourteenth Street in Manhattan, summoned no more excitement in their own hometown than they did anywhere else.

The members were too young to have experienced this erosion of the local firsthand, but they grasped its import; Zack Oden, for in-stance, noted that thanks to KEXP, they had sold more records in Seat-tle than at home. As music fans, certainly, they all recognized how the Internet shaped their own listening habits: the roaming for the new band that always lurks just around the corner. "There's two sides to that shit," Adam said, when I asked him about the Internet. "One side is it's a really wonderful way to discover all kinds of music. But then it also completely taints you. It makes you not enjoy music as long."

"It shortens your attention span," added Zack. "Because you can always access new stuff."

"Just like everything else, every day," said Adam, with resignation.

He and Anna were now drawing with colored pencils around the burnt holes in his shirt.

"What are you putting on your shirt?" asked Kenny.

"Wizard's fire, baby," said Adam. "That's what I was wounded by."

I asked Adam, finally, about the name Annuals, a question I had been turning over in my mind ever since I first heard of the band.

"Actually, I remember the moment that I thought of the word," Adam said. "I was coming home from school, and I was looking at one of my mom's flowers. And I had just, like, started recording my little side-project shit. And I thought: Annuals."

I felt relieved to learn that the name did not mean for him what it had come to mean for me, a melancholy vision of a beautiful band built, constitutionally, to die. I had begun to imagine all of my wanderings through rock clubs and festivals, through blogs and social networks and download sites, as the meanders of a floraphile through resplendent gardens that will flourish only for a season; to regard all these remarkable new bands, seemingly inexhaustible in supply, as dazzling marigolds, begonias, impatiens—their palettes brilliant but their roots fragile, incapable of abiding a frost. Indeed, in my fevered brain the word ANNUALS now hung above my whole dark mental tableau of viral culture, with its waves upon waves of showy, brave nanostories, the spikes supplanted unceasingly by more spikes, and it gave me a bit of hope to discover that for Adam, at least, the name still spoke to something gorgeous.

BEAUTIFUL IT-CHILDREN

Not long ago the *New York Times Book Review*, eager to court the hoopla that attends all media rankings of the unrankable, sent a letter to hundreds of prominent writers, critics, and editors, asking them each to pick the single best work of American fiction published in the previous twenty-five years. The results were compiled into the inevitable list. *Beloved*, by Toni Morrison, led the brass band, with Don DeLillo's *Underworld*, Cormac McCarthy's *Blood Meridian*, John Updike's Rabbit Angstrom quadrilogy, and Philip Roth's *American Pastoral* tromping up just behind. From the color commentary offered up in the *Times*'s companion essay, by the critic A. O. Scott, one factoid stood out: all five of these writers had been born in the span of just six years, between 1931 and 1936. And the gerontocracy was alarmingly absolute. Of the twenty-two works that received more than one vote, only four had been written by authors born after 1945, and none at all by authors born after 1951, an age distribution that looked like so:

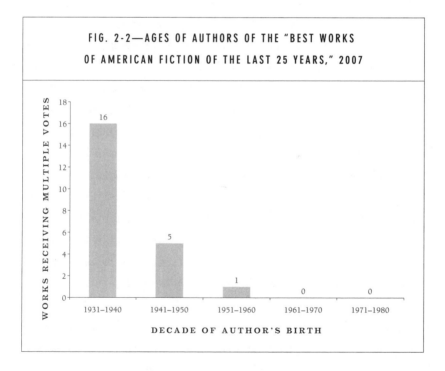

FIG. 2-2—AGES OF AUTHORS OF THE "BEST WORKS OF AMERICAN FICTION OF THE LAST 25 YEARS," 2007

"In sifting through the responses," Scott remarked, "I was surprised at how few of the highly praised, boldly ambitious books by younger writers—by which I mean writers under 50—were mentioned. One vote each for *The Corrections* and *The Amazing Adventures of Kavalier & Clay*, none for *Infinite Jest* or *The Fortress of Solitude*, a single vote for Richard Powers, none for William T. Vollmann, and so on." Almost entirely missing from our notions of "great," that is, was the work of an entire generation of well-established novelists (Franzen, Chabon, Wallace, Lethem, and the other writers Scott mentions, all of them born between 1959 and 1964) and also, one might add, a second entire generation of just-publishing writers, born in the 1970s, who were now coming along behind. One can hypothesize any number of comforting explanations for this absence (demography of the survey's eminent voters, the lack of time for young writers' reputations to harden), and yet the poll's verdict, while arguably incorrect on the merits, felt terribly *inevitable*—it seemed hard to imagine that the slighted novels and writers Scott listed would be judged by history as "great," in the sense with which we apply that word to Roth or Nabokov or James or Melville. The ineradicable defect lay not in the works and authors themselves but in how they had been presented to us, the way that An Important Novel by a Young Writer had, over that quarter-century, become something packaged and sold in a very particular fashion.

That is: as with indie-rock bands, the rapid appearance and disappearance of young writers is a byproduct of niche sensationalism, though in this case a sensationalism that has prevailed in the literary world for the past two decades. The basic problem can be traced back to roughly 1987, when the anointing by the *Village Voice* of a "literary brat pack" (including such writers as Jay McInerney, Bret Easton Ellis, and Tama Janowitz) created a new paradigm by which a first-time novelist could be assessed much like a pop singer or matinee idol. Ever since then, the young writer has come into the public consciousness in this and only this compromised fashion: he or she becomes the writer one must read *just then* not because his or her work is good, but because it represents something about the moment, or about the youthful cohort from which the writer sprung. Here is Frank Bruni, in his famously ex-ecrable feature-length profile of David Foster Wallace ("The Grunge American Novel") for the *New York Times Magazine* in 1996:

> The critics aren't the only ones angling to prove that they get it. Wallace's contemporaries have shown up at his public appear-ances in force. When he read at K.G.B., Elizabeth Wurtzel, the author of "Prozac Nation," claimed a spot near the front of the room. The following night, at another jampacked reading, this time at Tower Books in the Village, Ethan Hawke lurked in the back. And at the official book party two nights later at an East Village club, M. G. Lord, the author of "Forever Barbie," can be seen chatting up another novelist of the moment, A. M. Homes. Between puffs of their cigarettes, many people whisper what Wallace says he does not want to hear: he is the current "it" boy of contemporary fiction.

Infinite Jest came out a year before Roth's *American Pastoral*; but re-reading Bruni's tripe today we can understand why even as the latter book, the work of an older writer, could be immediately apprehended—as if from fifty years' distance—as a thing at least striving toward a kind of timelessness, we were forced for years to see the former, though in its actual printed text a far more ambitious and writerly and even pro-found work of art, as a defunct media phenomenon of its moment. Too many articles in 1996 told us how *cool* Wallace and his novel were for us to properly see either as *great.**

So it has been for all the waves and waves of piercingly yet fleetingly important young writers, ever since the literary brat pack strutted

---

* The only solace in Wallace's recent and senseless passing has been an overdue re-consideration of this.

around the New York of the media's imagination. A by no means exhaustive list of such writers would include not just the aforereferenced Franzen, Lethem, Wurtzel, Lord, and Homes, but also Donna Tartt, Rick Moody, Dave Eggers, Arthur Phillips, Zadie Smith, Jonathan Safran Foer, James Frey, Benjamin Kunkel, Marisha Pessl, and countless more in between. While Frank Bruni has been mercifully dispatched to the Dining desk, we may still rely on the *Times Magazine* to provide us, at regular intervals, with impeccably timed hyperventilation about some young novelist. At the time of this writing, it was one Charles Bock, a lean, attractive New Yorker who had published a novel about Las Vegas called *Beautiful Children*. The novel had taken Bock a harrowing eleven years to complete, and at thirty-eight, the magazine noted, he was "a little old to be a first novelist"; but nevertheless in the story's lead, the reporter (former *Times* book-review editor Charles McGrath) makes clear who this piece was really about and for: the gang from which Bock had graduated. "You can spot them in coffee shops in Brooklyn and the West Village, clicking away on their laptops—when they're not wasting time on Gawker, that is," McGrath wrote, in a particularly Brunian motion. "You also see them at readings at Housing Works, KGB Bar and the Half King, dressed in black, leaning forward intently and sometimes venturing to ask a probing question. They idolize Lethem, Chabon, Eggers." *They* are what make this piece important, the young writers as a class, standing in for young urbanites as a class, the inevitable appearance of the hipster throng serving to yoke the writer and his work to a particular demographic at a particular moment: portrait of the artist as instantiation of a trend.

Why does the media keep doing it to us—and to them? Why do reporters persist in coronating "it-boys" and (less often) "it-girls," asking them to stand in for a generation and an era, even though this act is utterly fatal to how a reading public will apprehend their work over time? One might even say that the it-children (to coin a collective gender-neutral noun) are killing literature, considering that since the mid-1980s, which whelped that first litter of them, the portion of Americans saying they had read a book of fiction in the previous six months has fallen by a fifth, from 57 percent to 47 percent. And yet the more plausible causation runs the other way. Literature has become such a niche obsession that the only way to publish stories about it is through niche sensationalism; a new writer who can speak to some lost demographic (usually the young) is the only thing in the little world of American letters that can be called big news. Moreover, in the career of a journalist, it-children play an especially important role, because they allow the reporter—who is usually older—to trump up a subject's youth appeal and thereby sponge off it, even as doing so begins to diminish that appeal. To explain a novel by reference to its "buzz," not to mention its author's invariably attractive and black-clad peers (always at KGB!), is both to bask in that imputed coolness oneself and to bootstrap oneself above it, to cast it as a perishable taste that the reporter can be seen sampling just before it dies. This follows the fundamental action of the media mind: to find the thing with momentum and latch on to it, redefining it, drawing some of its power onto you even as you weaken it. The media mind is about *parasitism*. And the paradigmatic act of media parasitism, one should always remember, is to sup vampirically at the neck of young, doomed fame. With that in mind, let us return to the story of Annuals.

A WEEK INSTEAD OF SIX MONTHS

The South by Southwest festival (aka SXSW), held each March in Austin, Texas, is the closest thing indie rock has to a national convention, a four-day caucus at which all the ambitious indie acts are expected to mount the dais. The number of acts at the festival has swelled to more than 1,500, performing on some sixty separate official stages, and this tally does not include the countless unofficial bands, on unofficial stages, hoping to be seen by the thousands of indie-industry functionaries who roam the streets with their all-access badges. Every alleyway or back patio of every club or store seemed to have a tent with a band blaring away underneath. The first, sleepy day of the festival, before most of the attendees had arrived, I found myself on Sixth Street, the main club drag, at dusk, where I floated almost alone down the cordoned-off thoroughfare; the strains of the bands in all the empty clubs all sluiced together into the street, a multitonal wash of noise around me, a Charles Ives score for a little ghost town.

KEXP had set up shop on the UT–Austin campus, broadcasting its in-studio appearances from the set of *Austin City Limits*, the venerable public-TV music show. I caught up with John Richards the following afternoon, a Thursday, shortly after he signed off his shift, and we sat down in a spare, lofty office just off the set. It had been only half a year since Richards and I first met, but I found him obsessed with an entirely new slate of bands. "It almost worries me that the burnout is going to happen in a week instead of six months," he said, only half joking. There was a wave of new British acts: pop-punk bands the Holloways and the Fratellis (the latter of which had just had their song "Flathead" turned into an iPod ad); the retro-soul songstress Amy Winehouse (who had not yet become the mainstream misfit); and Fujiya & Miyagi, a hypnotic and danceable electronic group. There were the other domestic bands of the moment, including Deerhunter, the Ponys, and Menomena, all smart, admirably difficult acts that had each released a couple of albums before but for some reason were just getting big now. Annuals did not come up.

The very first band Richards mentioned in his list, the band "at the top of their game," as Richards put it, was Peter Bjorn and John, a Swedish act best known for their song "Young Folks," a laid-back and likable dance number built on a dispiritingly addictive whistle riff:

FIG. 2-3—THE PETER BJORN AND JOHN WHISTLE RIFF

Peter Bjorn and John had built this simple figure into a cacophony of attention, by way of the typical channels. Pitchfork bestowed an 8.5 on the full album, *Writer's Block*, and then chose them to headline the website's own South by Southwest party—a spot that one could imagine almost any of the 1,500 bands would have accepted. KEXP put them on their live bill too; in fact, Peter Bjorn and John was the band I had come to see perform that day. They were scheduled for quarter to two in the afternoon, and I sat in the near-empty bleachers and watched them set up.

The stage set of *Austin City Limits* seemed, at first glance, like an incongruous backdrop for indie rock. A kitschily stylized Austin skyline in the evening, it managed to render a too-sleepy city even sleepier-seeming in miniature. For that matter, Peter, Bjorn, and John (their actual names) seemed an incongruous indie-rock trio, at least visually speaking: The first two, who have played together for a decade, were mop-topped, fashionably unkempt fellows in tight black jeans, whereas the third, the drummer, wore a suit jacket over a crisp, white dress shirt, his black hair impeccably styled to one side, his overall look resembling that of a villainous investment-banker in an '80s movie.* But

---

* I later discovered that he was not John at all, but rather a stand-in drummer named Nino, who fills in when John is off performing with his side project, a classical percussion ensemble.

stage and band seemed to come together fine when it all started up; the stands, which for the other bands that day had been half-empty or worse, were very much full.

Before I arrived in Austin, I realized that Annuals' season in the fickle sun had ended, and I found that my marvel at it all, at the ever-flowering garden of *good-enough bands,* had given way, I must confess, to a species of anger. Peter Bjorn and John, too, were good, yes, and so were these other bands, but what about the bands from six months ago—Annuals, but also White Whale, Bound Stems, Tokyo Police Club, bands whose names even you, unfaithful reader, perhaps have already forgotten from just a few pages prior? I had begun to forget them too. We falter like the others, don't we—enjoying the stories put in front of us today and forgetting the rest? How can we resist the new band, the new track, the one that everyone else is listening to, linking to, cueing up at parties? "Young Folks" was exactly that track, and as Peter Bjorn and John started in on it, I couldn't help but get a certain thrill despite myself, and the rest of the crowd clearly did too. Some teenagers, who earlier on had improbably bounded out from the wings to sit Indian-style before the stage, now rose to their feet and began to dance, as unselfconsciously as only teenagers are able to, and in the heartbreakingly loose-limbed style they seem to prefer. Peter, it must be said, could whistle with astonishing skill, performing the difficult riff over and over again without falter. *But wait*—halfway through, there is a malfunction; his lips unpurse and yet the riff goes on—*he has been lip-synching the whistle.* And now, acknowledging his mistake, Peter begins to laugh as he sings, and Bjorn begins to laugh too, and now John, as well, all cracking up at their mighty hit, cut off at the knees. I hurry to write it down in my notebook, because Peter Bjorn and John is my enemy, and their slipup will become an item on my blog.

EXPERIMENT: STOP PETER BJORN AND JOHN

Here I should be clear. I did not, and do not, have any particular dislike for Peter Bjorn and John or their music. But seeing that they clearly were poised to become the so-called buzz band of SXSW, that welling anger of mine—that desperate desire to stop Internet time, or at least to let the cycles last longer, let the spikes stretch wider—had focused, for the moment, on these affable Swedes. I began to chart out an experiment in viral culture that, unlike the flash mob, would explore nanostories purely in the negative; in this case, addressing the question of whether "buzz" could be self-consciously neutralized or reversed. On Wednesday, March 7, precisely one week before the festival began, I had created an anonymous blog, called Stop Peter Bjorn and John, which described itself as "an emergency blog to stop the spread of the Swedish band Peter Bjorn and John."

In a long introductory post that Friday, I laid out the case:

> [W]e are headed into SXSW with the serious danger that Peter Bjorn and John will be turned into the "buzz" or "breakout" band of the festival. . . . As much as we would all like to just ignore the whole "buzz band" phenomenon—to chalk it up (correctly) to the meaningless machinations of a press in need of a story—the fact is that those decisions matter. They matter in terms of what bands get played, what bands get signed, what bands get associated with indie rock as a genre. Whether we like it or not, the sound of the "buzz band" gets attributed to us, in terms of what we supposedly like. We, the indie-rock fans, suffer when the buzz band is bad. Which brings us to the question: Do we want Peter Bjorn and John to be hailed as the standard bearers for a whole genre of music? And the answer is: NO WAY. . . . "Young Folks" was catchy and harmless, but this band is *not a significant band.* Peter Bjorn and John must be stopped.

> And we can do it. . . . We make these bands ourselves, online,
> through our posts, listens, downloads, and links. If we want to
> take them down, we can.

This was precisely the theory that I thought the Stop Peter Bjorn and John experiment could address. I knew that Internet buzz was not only creating these waves and waves of short-lived bands, but was doing so in a basically arbitrary fashion: the Columbia music study (addressed in chapter 1) made this fact clear, that in terms of popular bands created in social networks, we were living in only one of many possible worlds. Which raised an important question: could *antibuzz* spread through the same channels as buzz, with correspondingly negative effects?

In retrospect, I concede that my experiment might not have been ideally designed. The centerpiece of the campaign was to be an anti–Peter Bjorn and John rally, held outside Austin's Waterloo Records on the following Friday at 3:00 p.m., when the band was slated to make an in-store appearance there. All attendees were to bring a sign, or wear a shirt, that expressed their feelings against the band. "What I plan to do," I wrote, "is write 'PBJ' on a piece of duct tape and put it over my mouth"—explaining in a parenthetical that "[t]he idea is that trying to make PBJ into a breakout band is essentially silencing those of us who hate the band." A fake "update" at the bottom of the post suggested that "30–40" people had already e-mailed me to say they would be attending, and I added enough fake comments to suggest this might be plausible.

Real commenters began to trickle in over that weekend, and then, at the beginning of the following week, bona fide nanonarrativity was achieved: on Monday the site was picked up by Gawker.com, and then by its sister music site, Idolator, and then, over the next few days, by the websites of *Entertainment Weekly*, the *Los Angeles Times*, *Mother Jones*, and *amNew York*, as well as numerous smaller blogs, the adoption/abandonment curve taking its familiar shape:

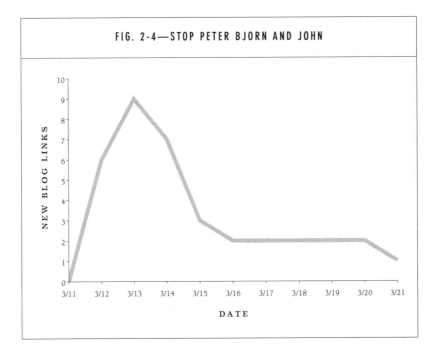

FIG. 2-4—STOP PETER BJORN AND JOHN

Stop Peter Bjorn and John had created buzz. But what, exactly, was the content of that buzz? Had it done anything to unsettle the trajectory of the band? Or was the site's buzz only for itself? A few signs were encouraging. First, the site seemed to be sowing uncertainty, in a Karl Rove–like strategy: the existence of the site meant that bloggers had to write about the band's ascendance not as a unanimous coronation but as a fraught matter. E.g., a blog called Lost in Texas, on 3/12: "Are Peter, Bjorn, and John the newest idol of the American music scene, a la Sufjan Stevens? Or is this blog right, and PB&J need to be stopped?" From the Live-Journal of 14icedbear: "i happen to tentatively like pb&j (tentatively because i haven't really heard all that much of them yet), but i do understand being frustrated by the monumental success of a band you find to be mediocre." Best of all, the *San Francisco Chronicle*'s culture blog linked to the site offhandedly in calling Peter Bjorn and John "controversial."

This true antibuzz for the band, however, was overwhelmed by antibuzz for me—or, I should say, for the character of the anonymous blogger I had created. I had tried hard to develop him as a tragic figure, a man utterly undone by his gnawing hatred for Peter Bjorn and John. He drives from his hometown (which remains unspecified) to Austin, even though the trip will take two solid days. On the first night of the festival, he makes an elaborate plan of the bands he wants to see—noting that he will be sure to avoid the club where Peter Bjorn and John are playing. The next day, though, he confesses that he walked by the club despite himself, and the large turnout threw him into a spiral of rage that wound up ruining his entire evening.

But among readers, sympathy for his anguish proved elusive. Commenters steadily slung epithets against me (him), beginning with "dipshit" and "fuckface" and then going on from there: "wanker," "asshat," "douchebag," "pretentious douchebag," "obnoxious hipster douchebag." "People like you are dumb," one commenter opined.

The source of the animosity was, I admit, unclear to me. My antagonists seemed to object to (a) my negativity and (b) the leisure time I apparently had to create the blog, and so they expended leisure time of their own to deliver negativity against me in return. A somewhat more coherent expression of this backlash came from commenter "Jim," who wrote, "Get a freaking life already will ya? Are you aware there's a war going on? And you're going to protest A BAND!?"

In a subsequent post, I wrote a reply to Jim. If protesting a band during a war was a waste of time, I asked, then why should one bother to *support* a band during wartime, either? I went on:

> The obvious answer is: because you still think culture is important. But if you think culture is important, then you need not just to support the bands you like but oppose the bands that need to be opposed.

There was a clear hole in my argument, though. My opposing a band seemed to have supported it. Even the band thought so. While onstage during a day party in Austin, on the first day of the festival, Peter Bjorn and John thanked Stop Peter Bjorn and John. I was not there, but I am told they even read out the URL.

EASE MY MIND

Annuals was there too, at South by Southwest. As all the bands with any reputation did, they played multiple shows, of which I saw the first and the last. At the first, in a tented patio adjoining a bar, they shared the bill with a band called Illinois, a dreamily ramshackle, banjo-driven rock act that was just then in the throes of blowup: Idolator, in fact, that very week dissected Illinois' buzz in almost identical fashion to their post about Annuals six months prior, down to the same cynical "Odds of Backlash"—5:1. The tent filled for Illinois, but most of the crowd stayed for Annuals, and what they saw was, as ever, magnificent.

The last Annuals show of the festival I happened upon by chance, as I walked with my wife up Trinity Street. The band was loading equipment from their big white van into the Austin Convention Center, where they were to tape a few songs for a radio station. While they waited to go on, we all lay around on the floor in the main corridor, a sunny, echoing plate-glass atrium some sixty feet high and three football fields long. Another show had been booked for that night, but news of its cancellation arrived while we chatted. I never saw a band so happy to have a gig scotched. The drive back to Raleigh would take twenty-five hours, and they intended to do it straight through.

They hoped it would be a trip back, if only briefly, to their other projects: the other bands they wanted to be. They had a two-week break, and they were finally going to use it to record as Sedona—Kenny's band, the band they'd been before Annuals got signed. Adam wanted to finish a few songs for Tundra. "And we might start on BandAnd—" he added, then noticed my quizzical look and explained: BandAnd was a hard-rock band, to be run by Zack.

"I think that'll have to be on our next break," Zack averred.

"It's like avant-garde metal fusion, pretty much," Kenny said.

"It's all of us trying to be as technical and heavy as possible," Zack said.

"We've got, like, little riffs that we've written for it," Kenny said. "We haven't put anything together fully, but we've got a lot of ideas."

The last song Annuals played in the taping was one I'd never heard them do live: a sublimely meditative track called "Ease My Mind." Kenny had written it; he sang lead vocals and played a blistering acoustic. Where Annuals, lyrically, was achingly broken, this song was elliptically spiritual. It was not an Annuals song, even though it was becoming that. It was a Sedona song: the same thing but another thing entirely. Annuals might have been the perfect name for them, I realized, but in a different way from what I thought. Maybe their destiny was to be a march of bands in themselves, not one fuchsia in the frost, but a thousand blooming in succession. Maybe they would learn to make art, to find narrative, in this churning, viral culture by embodying the churn, embracing it, by envisioning a life not as some decades-long epic, but as a succession of discretely plotted six-month shorts.

MOB #9 (OF A SORT)

At quarter till three, my wife and I took a cab to Waterloo Records for the Stop Peter Bjorn and John event. We had no duct tape, no shirts, no signs. If a protest had materialized, we would have been mere spectators to it. The store was a long and low-slung building, a single story painted fern green on top and sky blue below. In the narrow parking lot in front, people were milling about: were they protesters? We wandered among them; none of them had signs either. There was a TV news van, its antenna hoisted promisingly for signal, but we could see that the reporters were all inside the store, covering the show. We saw a police officer, too; an echo of MOB #1? But she was eating an ice-cream cone, paying no heed to us or to anyone else.

We walked around the corner and loitered. At five till, two U-Haul vans pulled up beside us, and Peter, Bjorn, and John all emerged, looking as weary as I did. Bjorn brushed something off the shoulder of his black shirt before putting his jacket on over it, and then the three strode around to the front, through the growing line (for that is what the milling people had become, not a problem but a pliant queue), and into the store. Not a single protester had shown up. It was somewhat as I expected. At the stroke of 3:00 p.m., I had arranged for a farewell post to be added to the Stop Peter Bjorn and John blog. It began:

> To those of you who are turning up right now to protest: I am sorry. This whole campaign against Peter Bjorn and John has pushed me to what I now realize is a total mental and emotional breakdown. . . . I simply can't carry this burden any longer. I have packed up my car and am leaving town.

As an experiment in viral culture, Stop Peter Bjorn and John had been both a failure and a success. It had failed, of course, to stop the band in question, which left SXSW as popular as ever. (Their oblivion did not arrive for roughly another two months.) I could see now what was meant by the maxim that all publicity is good publicity. In chapter 1, I wrote about "backlash," as if active hate of something can stop its cultural ascent. But if I can take any lesson from my antibuzz blog, and from my months of subcultural wanderings in general, it is that backlash is about not hate but *boredom,* about attention no longer paid or extended, about an arc of a story completed. Hate only extends that arc, prolonging a story through controversy; spikes cannot be unspiked through stimulation but only through distraction or forgetting. Like the students in that classic boredom study, we imagine a band (or book, or idea) to be boring only because we hear the next already playing in the other room, slowly turning up its amps. To hate a meme only makes it stronger, if only for a few more moments until it, ignored, expires.

However: Stop Peter Bjorn and John had succeeded, if somewhat modestly, as an Internet meme of its own. It had emerged ex nihilo and found a sizeable audience within a single week. Antibuzz had not worked to stop buzz, but it had built buzz of its own, selling a peculiar brand of bitterness to adherents and detractors as well, all of whom paid repeated visits. If creating memes is a craft, then false controversy is a key ratchet in its chest of tools.

As it happens, there are many other wrenches to master. In chapter 3, we will examine the nascent craft of pure meme-making—that is, the creation of viral culture for no reason other than to see it spread—its growing crowd of practitioners, and the singular pleasures (and profits) to be found in this peculiarly twenty-first-century pursuit.

3.

I HAVE A MEME

EXPERIMENT: THE RIGHT-WING *NEW YORK TIMES*

MEME MACHINE

As our online culture is built, more and more, on short-lived sensations, this in turn changes how we *make* culture. How could it not? When one blog post (or MySpace song, or YouTube video) attracts ten times more traffic, or a hundred times more traffic, than all the others do, how can we help but scrutinize the popular one, hoping to divine some rules behind its sway? By the grace of the Internet's constant churn, we are presented with an unending stream of such successes: every hour brings new tiny nanostories, little contagious spikes, to analyze and interpret and understand. This phenomenon is especially vivid on the "collaboratively filtered" information sites, communities where content is presented in ranked lists based on the real-time whims of the hive-mind; the three largest of these (Reddit, del.icio.us, and especially Digg) each can drive tens or even hundreds of thousands of visitors to the day's top sites, leaving content creators to dream up the right formula—aka "Diggbait"—to draw the hordes in their direction.

Thus does online culture grope toward a particular sort of ideal: a meme ideal. And thus do culture-makers take on a new and distinctly contemporary role. They become what Richard Dawkins, following the meme/gene parallel to its natural conclusion, called "memetic engineers," amateur experts who calibrate how to conceive, launch, and promote memes so as best to ensure their propagation. Some of the new engineering techniques are designed to operate on single terms, such as the "Google bomb"—a technique where confederated websites all collude to try to create a particular top ranking on a Google search. This technique was used by opponents of George W. Bush in making his official White House page come up as the top search result for the phrase "miserable failure"; similarly for Tony Blair and the word "liar." After the former senator Rick Santorum delivered some appallingly homophobic remarks in an interview, his surname was turned into a sexual slang word, which a Google search for his last name today— long after he lost his reelection bid—still returns as the number-one result. Similar campaigns have been launched to create DIY memes, with the goal not just of conquering a Google term but of advancing an idea or selling oneself. Dan Savage, editor of the alt-weekly *The Stranger* and originator of the "santorum" campaign, also tried to start an anti-Bush meme called ITMFA (Impeach That Motherfucker Already), with results that one can only call mixed: it currently gets 118,000 results on Google, but as of this writing the MF remained regrettably un-I'ed.*

---

* This engineering spirit has been with us since the Internet's early days. In a famous 1990 project, a lawyer named Mike Godwin, who had grown tired of how readily online antagonists stooped to accuse one another of being "similar to the Nazis" or "Hitler-like," created a "countermeme" that he called Godwin's Law. The official language of the law was this: "As an online discussion grows longer, the probability of a comparison involving Nazis or Hitler approaches one." The

As commerce and culture have increasingly migrated online, the stakes in memetic engineering have heightened considerably, and our experiments have become less idle, more pointed. Every month we see new viral sensations, personalities like Ze Frank (host of his own online video show) or Amanda Congdon (from a news video site called Rocketboom) or Jessica Rose (the actress-star of the Lonelygirl15 videos), who parlay Internet stardom into a version of the real thing, and we scheme about how their path to fame might become our own. We see collaborative product sites like Threadless.com, where T-shirt designs compete to be sold every week, with the winning designers awarded $2,000—ample incentive to try our own hand at giving the voters what they want. Our engineering instincts take more idealistic directions, too, of course: for example, we see political sites that succeed, as have Talking Points Memo on the left and Power Line on the right during the past few years, in rallying evidence to oppose various government policies or media narratives, and so we set out to make our own memes and countermemes for advancing our own political purposes.

What spreads we then imitate, amplify, anatomize, satirize; and some of what we thereby create spreads as well, providing us with more data to analyze and giving other meme-makers one more example to emulate. Together we are engineering a meme-making machine, which hour by hour entertains and even enriches us as its ultimate effects on our culture remain unclear.

---

real intent of the law, of course, was simply to shame: comparing one's enemy to the Nazis, he was saying, is almost always so overheated and clichéd as to be not only offensive but useless. He set about seeding his countermeme in any discussion group where he came across an unnecessary Nazi reference. It quickly spread, to the point that such references were actively pilloried in online forums. Even today, to make a Nazi analogy online is to risk finding oneself on the receiving end of Godwin's Law.

THE CONTAGIOUS FESTIVAL

For just over a year, there was a curious monthly contest that embodied precisely this emergent vision of culture. It was called the Contagious Festival, although "festival" was decidedly euphemistic, because what happened each month was a rather hard-nosed competition. Its rules were simple: create the website that gets the most visitors, and win $2,500. A second "jury prize," of an equal amount, was also given out afterward, but the popularity contest was the marquee event. The contest's sponsor, the left-leaning news site the Huffington Post, provided the server space for free. Entries could be launched anytime during the month; entrants could promote their site, or not, in any way they so chose (short of sending out spam). And the winner, quite simply, was whichever site got the most visitors. All that mattered was your number—no matter how sophisticated or mawkish or juvenile your site, no matter which type of media it was plying.

Over the course of the year, top-ten finishers ranged from simple drawings to music files to videos to elaborate combinations of every medium. Most entries tended to be stabs at humor, but some successful sites took stridently dark or somber tones—one antiwar song had garnered more than 500,000 views. Because of the Huffington Post's politics, most entries tended to include a left-wing message, but not all: in the Festival's first month, one of the top-ranked sites was "Awwwwstrich," a quick-cut music video of rapping ostriches. Some of the entries were funny, or at least clever and well put-together, but quality clearly did not determine a site's performance. The primary criterion was that it *hit*, i.e., compelled a reader to pass it along, and isolating this ineffable quality was the goal toward which the competitors strove.

The mastermind behind the Contagious Festival was Jonah Peretti, the Huffington Post's technology director and one of its founders. Jonah, at thirty-two, embodied precisely those qualities that this decade has conspired to produce in its high-status young men: savvy in matters technological, and yet charismatic, articulate, fashionably dressed, nice teeth. He wore distressed blue jeans and chunky designer glasses. Late one July, just before the start of the August competition, I visited him at the Huffington Post's offices in SoHo, and even the space displayed his blend of tech-company informality and fastidious *début de siècle* style: in one room, Warhol prints lined the wall, even as the desks were crammed together uncomfortably along the perimeter to make room for a pool table. My intention was to cover the Contagious Festival for the month of August, in order to witness, in real time, the blowup of a manufactured Internet meme; to observe some new advancement, however small, in the emergent science—and sport—of cultural manipulation. I wanted to meet with Jonah beforehand, not only because he was the contest's ringmaster but because he himself was a memetic engineer of the highest order.

Jonah had fallen into the world of meme-making somewhat by accident. After college, he taught for three years in New Orleans and then shipped off to graduate school at the Massachusetts Institute of Technology's Media Lab, a sort of tech-wizard Wonka factory where students envision and enact bold new uses for computing technology. While writing this thesis—his project was a straightforwardly earnest online database through which teachers nationwide could share lesson plans and advice—he played a joke that radically changed the course of his intellectual life. When Nike, the shoe manufacturer, unveiled a new "Nike iD" sales campaign in which consumers could customize their shoes with a word of their choice, Jonah decided to see if they would sell him shoes bearing the word "sweatshop." The answer: no. A Nike representative averred, in an e-mail, that the word violated the rule against "inappropriate slang." Jonah replied:

After consulting Webster's Dictionary, I discovered that "sweatshop" is in fact part of standard English, and not slang. The word means: "a shop or factory in which workers are employed for long hours at low wages and under unhealthy conditions" and its origin dates from 1892. So my personal iD does meet the criteria detailed in your first email.

Your web site advertises that the NIKE iD program is "about freedom to choose and freedom to express who you are." I share Nike's love of freedom and personal expression. The site also says that "If you want it done right . . . build it yourself." I was thrilled to be able to build my own shoes, and my personal iD was offered as a small token of appreciation for the sweatshop workers poised to help me realize my vision.

At the end of the exchange, what Jonah had in his possession was not, sadly, a pair of SWEATSHOP Nikes, but something arguably better: the e-mail exchange itself, which wittily exposed Nike's promotion as the soulless sham it was. He forwarded the exchange to roughly a dozen of his friends, and was shocked when, within weeks, he was receiving inquiries from national media about it. His e-mail exchange had spread to literally millions of readers around the world. He was invited to appear on the *Today* show to debate a Nike executive.

Now Jonah was not so interested in his thesis anymore. "All of a sudden, I was spending all my time walking around MIT, asking people about how media spreads through networks," he recalled when we sat down to chat on a stylishly modern sofa at the Huffington Post. At the Media Lab, he was perfectly situated to put some hard science to this question. The first relevant discipline, Jonah discovered, was the science of networks—"how many connections you need between each node for it to be possible for something to become contagious, how do different network structures affect the spread of information, and questions like that." The second was cognitive science: "When an individual who's a node in the network encounters a piece of media, how do they make a decision? How do they decide whether they pass it along to all of their friends, whether they're outraged, whether they're inspired, whether they're sad, whether they take action, or don't take action?"

After graduating from MIT, Jonah moved to New York and embarked on further contagious adventures. In collaboration with his sister Chelsea, a stand-up comic, he created the Rejection Line, a Manhattan telephone number that New York singles could hand out to undesirable suitors, who would call to receive the bad news from an automated recording (in Jonah's voice): "Welcome to New York City's Rejection Line. The person who gave you this number does not want to talk to you, or speak to you, again. I would like to take this opportunity to officially reject you. . . . " They also created a site called BlackPeopleLoveUs.com, which purported to be the home page of a white couple, Sally and Johnny, boasting about how many black friends they have. As evidence, the black friends have left testimonials. "Sally loves to touch my hair!" one says. "Johnny calls me 'da man!' " says another.

Jonah's central insight was that sites spread when they speak to the particular relationships between people. There needs to be, in Jonah's words, "a social hook to the media." At the time of our interview, for example, the number-one most e-mailed story on the *New York Times* site was entitled "What Shamu Taught Me About a Happy Marriage," and in it the author applied the techniques of a dolphin trainer to understanding and controlling her husband. The piece had spread, Jonah pointed out, because it had an obvious social hook. "People are going to send that to their spouse—ha-ha, right?—or they're going to send it to their girlfriend if they've been talking about relationships, et cetera." Black People Love Us was the same way: "It's about race relations, so black people are going to share it with their white friends, or vice versa. There's a social imperative to it, and so that social imperative makes you share it with other people, because you want to talk to them about it."

EXPERIMENT: THE RIGHT-WING *NEW YORK TIMES*

Jonah and I agreed that I would cover the August competition, tracking the twists and turns of the tally and getting to know some of the contestants along the way. Often the entries were made under pseudonyms, and so he offered to help put me in touch with the real meme-makers behind the sites. There was, however, one dimension of my project that I did not disclose to Jonah, or to the contestants I would interview: so as better to understand the dynamics of the competition, I had decided to enter it myself. For a pseudonym, I settled on "Will Murphy"—not a flat-out lie, I reasoned, since "Murphy" is my wife's surname and "Will" is a fair substitute for "Bill" (one I had even considered adopting in college, during an unfortunately preppy phase).

Using Jonah's advice, I set out three basic conditions that my entry needed to satisfy. First and most crucially, it should speak directly to the primary audience, the group of people who would be the first to see it—in this case the readers of the Huffington Post, which provided the first-line viewership for the whole competition. Any entry that hoped to spread would need to excite these core readers, creating a conversation that fit within their community, because outside readers were unlikely to find it in great enough numbers to build critical mass. And because the Huffington Post community, like those that have organized around the Daily Kos or Atrios or other left-leaning blog sites, existed entirely for the amplification of left-wing (or, more precisely, anti–right-wing) sentiments, a winning entry would have to dip at least a toe in that particular pool.

Second—and here was where things got a bit more complicated— the entry would eventually need to break out of its primary audience in order to truly blow up. It would need, that is, to show some crossover potential, so it could speak to a larger audience when the time came. The history of the competition was littered with third- or fifth-place finishers that had ignited the base but lacked a broad enough appeal to gain wider Internet celebrity. Jonah had made basically this point during our interview: "The question is, when do you make something that breaks out of the community that's supposed to react to it?" Black PeopleLoveUs.com had been aided in its spread by links on white supremacist sites, of all places.

As the subject for my own site, I chose the right wing's contempt for the *New York Times*, a hatred that had just then thickened to Homeric wrath after the newspaper had played a hand in uncovering two questionable Bush administration programs of domestic surveillance. For weeks right-wing pundits and bloggers had been in the throes of anti-*Times* apoplexy. My thought was: What if one could, as if through some magic psychological power, show what conservatives thought as they read the *Times*? Over the course of an afternoon I wrote it out. The premise was simple enough: the website would look just like the *Times*'s, but when a reader moved his mouse over a story, it would transform into a paranoid right-wing reading of the same article. For example, mousing over this story—

QUESTIONS SURFACE ABOUT
U.S. SURVEILLANCE PROGRAM

Sources at the NSA and FBI questioned the constitutionality and also the efficacy of the program, which placed hidden cameras in the urinals of U.S. falafel restaurants.

—would yield this:

COME KILL US, TERRORIST COMRADES!

Here is the treasonous revelation of the latest brilliant U.S. surveillance program, so that terrorists have an easy shot at massacring us—in this case, through anthrax-laced falafel nuggets.

SS | AND THEN THERE'S THIS

And so on.

To try to reach different audiences, I tried to write different types of jokes for the site that would appeal to different audiences. Some jokes— such as the one cited above—were designed to appeal to liberals, by ridiculing right-wing hatred of the *Times* and of "the media" in general. In another such joke, the mouseover simply added a sentence; here is the before:

150 IRAQIS KILLED AS
SECTARIAN VIOLENCE WIDENS

An attack in a crowded market, seemingly aimed at Shiites, was one of ten separate acts of violence today in Baghdad alone.

and the after:

150 IRAQIS KILLED AS
SECTARIAN VIOLENCE WIDENS

An attack in a crowded market, seemingly aimed at Shiites, was one of ten separate acts of violence today in Baghdad alone. By reporting this entirely true information, we hope to sap America's fighting spirit!

Unlike this first type of joke, which was designed to reach out to the core Huffington Post audience, the second type of joke was more straightforwardly anarchic: simple irony with no political agenda. In these jokes, the caricature of right-wing views was pushed to such an extent that what really was being ridiculed was the caricature itself, as in the case where a generic Dining headline (IN SEARCH OF THE PERFECT PAELLA) became COOKING WITH PLACENTAS AND COCAINE. Other similar jokes included this Sports headline—

CLINTONS PLAY SOCCER

WITH SEVERED HEAD OF VINCE FOSTER

—or, for that matter, the alternate title for the newspaper itself, which was dreamed up and added by my friend Brian, who so graciously and brilliantly engineered the site for me:

The Al-Qaeda Newsletter
(and Coupon Book)

My inclusion of the third type of joke, I admit, was shooting the moon, from a contagious-media point of view; but in the interests of science I figured I should make the attempt. This third type of joke consisted of *actual parodies of the* Times *from a conservative perspective;* i.e., these jokes could be taken as evidence that the point of the parody was in fact the opposite of its nominal point. Examples of such jokes could be seen in this headline from Metro, which mocked the *Times*'s reflexive pro-government slant on urban social services:

CITY TAX INCREASE FAILS

TO SEIZE ALL INCOME

or its sanctimoniousness on social issues in Sports:

YANKEES WIN, DESPITE HAVING

NO TRANSSEXUAL PLAYERS

Noting the contradictions among these three different joke types, a reader might have chalked it up to incoherence. But in fact it was a product of contagious engineering. One might call these joke types A, B, and –A, and though they shade into one another, they roughly break down as follows:

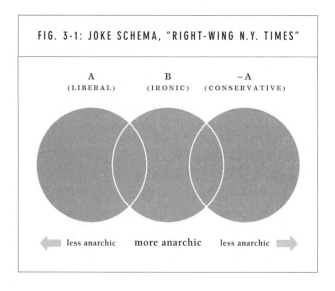

FIG. 3-1: JOKE SCHEMA, "RIGHT-WING N.Y. TIMES"

A
(LIBERAL)

B
(IRONIC)

–A
(CONSERVATIVE)

less anarchic   more anarchic   less anarchic

According to my hypothesis, these three different types of jokes, though disharmonious in certain aesthetic respects, would work together to spread the site—"What Right-Wingers See When They Read the *New York Times*," as it was officially called, the rendering of which Brian finished in the early morning of August 1, just as the competition was getting under way—with a three-prong approach. First, enough core Huffington Post readers would become excited about the A jokes that it would become circulated in the left-wing blogosphere. Second, its B jokes—its anarchic, purely comedic elements—would then propel it out into the wider circle of blogs and e-mail traffic. Third, its –A jokes, hopefully subtle enough not to interfere with the A jokes, would actually find it a foothold in the conservative blogosphere as well, possibly convincing right-wing readers that "Will Murphy" was, at heart, one of them.

VIRAL JUNKIES

Does any pleasure more define our age than the thrill of unleashing an Internet meme? One has created, at negligible cost and in minimal time, something entirely new—a gag Amazon review or a Photoshopped hoax image; a new song for one's MySpace account or, for one's blog, some new and cleverly contrarian line of political argument. One has laid it at the doorstep of literally the entire world, rung the bell, and run. Who will answer? In the bushes, giddy, one watches who, and how many, take the bait—by way of hit counters, server logs, comment threads, Google and Technorati searches for links. Two viral marketing experts I met both (literally at once) used the phrase "crack cocaine" to describe how it feels to track the stats on a contagious project, and during the Contagious Festival, I immediately saw what they meant. I took many hits from that particular pipe myself.

The drug metaphor is perhaps more apt than anyone would realize. Since the mid-1990s, psychologists have begun to identify some web-obsessed patients as sufferers of "Internet addiction disorder," which is believed to affect some 2 percent of Internet users worldwide; a 2007 Stanford study indicated that one in eight Americans may have a level of Internet use that is, if not a sign of addiction, at least "problematic." Much of the compulsive behavior centers around multiplayer online games, the most prominent of which, World of Warcraft, has more than ten million active subscribers. Nick Yee, a social scientist at the Palo Alto Research Center, surveyed more than three thousand such gamers about how their play had affected their lives. The results were startling. "I have played the game for 10 hours continuously or more"—more than half of players in all age ranges, male and female, said yes to this statement. "I would consider myself addicted to the game"—more than two-fifths overall, and two-thirds of boys aged twelve to seventeen, agreed. "I become anxious, irritable, or angry if I am unable to play"—more than 15 percent of the gamers copped even to this. One can appreciate why the government of China, always at the forefront of authoritarian social engineering, sends its young Internet fiends to military-style boot camps for detox.

To my knowledge, there are no scientific surveys as of yet on the addictiveness of Internet meme-making. But one might make a comparison to compulsive gambling, another pursuit in which a wager is made and the results are then obsessively tracked. On this subject, mental-health professionals have compiled extensive research. Robert Breen, a psychologist at the Rhode Island Hospital, has conducted multiple studies to demonstrate that machine gamblers—betters on slot machines, video poker machines, etc.—become pathological far more quickly than do devotees of other types of gambling. Indeed, his intriguing discovery was that games of chance seem to be more addictive in direct proportion to the rapidity and continuity of their "action"— how quickly, that is, a gambler is able to learn the outcome of his wager and then make another:

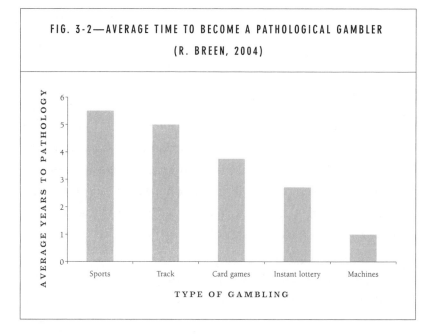

FIG. 3-2—AVERAGE TIME TO BECOME A PATHOLOGICAL GAMBLER
(R. BREEN, 2004)

Based on this insight, I fear that meme-making may be every bit the "crack" it is alleged to be. Certainly that was my own experience during those early days of August. With $2,500 on the line and visitor totals updated nearly in real time, I found myself refreshing the results page as often as every ten minutes. Between frantic reloads of that page, I of course had to check Technorati, too, to see if any blogs had linked to my site and, if so, what they had to say. Then there was the e-mail address listed on the site, which had to be checked too, for the torrents of fan mail I expected to pour in. At work, I kept a window open for each of these so I could easily refresh them. At home, I found myself straying constantly toward the laptop. If I woke in the middle of the night to use the bathroom, one thought would suddenly pierce my grog: *check the stats.* They moved slowly, but even small numbers were mesmerizing to watch creep up. By August 2, already 104 people had visited my site, and by the next day, 501—more people than had come to even my biggest flash mob, and probably more than I could claim personally to know.

WEEK ONE

My first pang of competitive anxiety arrived on August 3, when I noticed the appearance of a new entry by none other than Ava Lowery, whom I knew by her formidable reputation: a media-savvy, fifteen-year-old antiwar wunderkind from Alabama, whose websites, which generally consisted of mournful slideshows of dead Iraqis set to music, came with a built-in and enthusiastic following. She had gotten death threats from her neighbors and an interview on CNN. Her new site for the competition, entitled "Letter to America!," was essentially a polemical mix tape: an indictment of the Bush administration in words and images, accompanied by catchy clips of pop songs. In my capacity as a professional journalist, I called Ava and talked to her about how she got started in meme-making.

"During the 2004 election," she told me, in the astonishingly precise, self-possessed tone that some TV-ready children are somehow able to muster, "I decided to start my own website and blog so that I could start voicing my *opinion*. You know, I'm a kid"—she pronounced this "*kee*-yud"—"and I was a lot younger at the time." Now, though, she dreamed big. "I think that online blogging and animations and that type of thing are becoming the new media," she said, by which she meant replacing the traditional media of television, print, and such. "It's by real people! It's not made by people who are getting paid to do what they do."

Like a Southern politician (which, I kept thinking as we talked, she may very well become someday) she offered a homespun analogy to explain why Internet media-makers had a vitality that their offline counterparts didn't. "You know, down South we're really into football. And like they say: once you go to the pros, people don't have the passion that they had in college." She was so sweet about it, I didn't even (as a self-declared professional journalist) take offense at it. What did offend me was my suspicion that her entry was going to wipe the field with mine.

This fear was confirmed on August 4, by the end of which I was in seventh place to her sixth. Even worse, the competition also saw its first case of bona fide contagion, which left both of our entries reeling far below. A short video lampooning the Bush administration's anti-marijuana policy—"Get Off the Pot, George"—began to move, and kept going over the next few days:

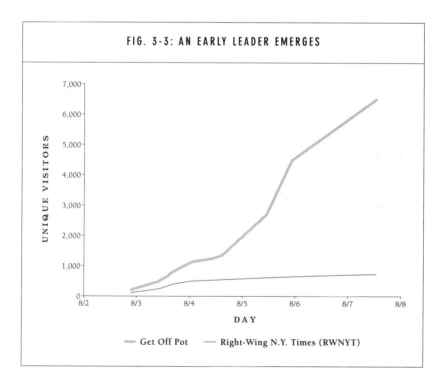

FIG. 3-3: AN EARLY LEADER EMERGES

By August 7, "Get Off the Pot" had won more than twice as many viewers as the nearest competitor, and nearly ten times my own. In my journalistic capacity, I called Jeff Meyers, the creator of "Get Off the Pot," and found a man rather pleased with himself.

"I never expected to be in first place, and so I'm not complaining," he said. Jeff was sixty and lived in Southern California, where for years he had worked a reporter and editor at the *Los Angeles Times*. In the late 1990s, he began suffering from arm and wrist pain—brought on, he said, by "the hunt-and-peck method of typing"—which led him to a political cause.

"I would go home at lunchtime and get high," he recalled. Not only could he then work through the pain, but he suddenly had all this energy—"I didn't get tired in the afternoon. So I became a real medical marijuana advocate." He took a buyout to retire from the *Times* in 1996, and a few years later codirected, with a fellow marijuana activist who made TV commercials, a pro-pot documentary entitled *Emperor of Hemp*. "Get Off the Pot" was in part an advertisement for the film, and when I asked him which goal was driving him—political change or product promotion—his answer seemed as noble as one could possibly expect.

"I wanted to get the political message out there, and inform people of the facts as I see them. My main goal was definitely to get the word out there. But did I think I might sell a few DVDs out of it? Maybe."

Have you sold any? I asked.

No, he said.

The spread of his Festival entry, though, did seem in line with Jonah's basic precept: contagious sites play on social relationships. Whatever one thought of the humor value of "Get Off the Pot"—which involved a poorly made puppet of George W. Bush sitting on a toilet—who among us has not known a "pot person," someone who vocally advertises his or her ongoing and frequent association with the drug? As I saw Meyers's numbers float steadily upward, I glumly imagined the vast underground network of stoners into whose bloodstream his entry had begun to circulate. I, meanwhile, was stuck in ninth place, with little prospect of getting higher.

THE ACCIDENTAL ORACLE

In second place, just behind "Get Off the Pot," was a rather odd entry entitled "How Do They Keep Cheney Alive?" Unlike almost all the other contenders, this was an entirely static page, with no video, animation, or even hyperlinks to burrow into. It took the pose of a parody advice columnist, named the Accidental Oracle, who answered the question posed in the site's title. His response, in part:

> How is the Vice President kept alive through all his heart attacks and other ailments?
>
> With fresh organs from the War on Terror.
>
> The organs are harvested from dying insurgents and terrorists, then flown fresh daily from the Middle East to a secret medical facility in Virginia.

The Accidental Oracle, as it happened, lived in the Williamsburg neighborhood of Brooklyn, just a few subway stops across the river from my office. His real name was Kurt Strahm, and he made his home in a pristinely kept building in the Polish part of town. He had once been an abstract artist of considerable promise, a fact that became evident as soon as I walked into his apartment and saw the work hanging throughout. Ghostly strands swam, on one canvas, in a sublime acrylic murk; down another, a cibachrome print, bands of color slid to dissolve, at bottom right, into a chemical scar, as if the developing reagents had rebelled partway through. In the painting above his computer desk, a wistful pattern ran like droplets across a rusty, translucent pane. Strahm is a fastidious man, probably in his early fifties (he declined to give his exact age), tall and slender with wavy gray hair combed back, a salt-and-pepper goatee, silver oval glasses. He dressed simply: a gray pocket-T, jeans, Teva sandals. His apartment was dustless and spare, the sort of immaculate, uncluttered space that most New Yorkers inhabit only in dreams, from which they awake heartbroken into their cramped real-life hovels.

"I started painting," said Strahm, who speaks in an even, caustic tone, "and then I lost interest, because there wasn't much to think about. I like my paintings just fine, but there *really* wasn't much to think about." He had grown up in California, in the Bay Area, and had gone to art school there. "I had a few solo shows in San Francisco, and that felt kind of empty; and then I got here and I met all these artists— I didn't really know any artists at all till I got here. And then I knew so many artists that I didn't want to know any more artists." The prestigious Brooklyn gallery Pierogi had given him a solo show in 2001, and the capsule review in the *Times*, which I looked up later, called it "flinty and ingenious." But today, aside from the occasional small computer- or video-based piece, Strahm was devoting himself to his work on the web. In addition to his own personal blog, called Restless, he kept up another recurring blog as the Accidental Oracle, which was devoted mostly to waging meme war against the right wing. ("You have to use entertainment, and satire and ridicule, and just, you know, let the fuckers on the right have it directly," he told me.) His August entry into the Festival was his third in as many months, all of them in the Accidental Oracle format. He previously had begun the title of each entry with the greeting "Dear Oracle."

"I thought if they liked one, they might like a series of them—they would recognize the name and come back," Strahm said. "But they don't do that." This is a common meme-maker's lament: viral projects spread through decontextualized blog links and e-mail forwards, and so viewers tend to pay no attention whatsoever to the domains that actually host the material—they never learn anything about the creators who entertain them. In the Internet circus, a seemingly infinite cast of clowns, daredevils, and freaks each step into the spotlight, enthrall the crowd for thirty seconds or so, and then exit back into the dark with barely a bow.

The project Strahm seemed most eager to show me was a sophisticated database he had built to categorize all of his viable ideas, so that they could eventually find their way onto his blog. At that point there were 201 entries that had made the cut ("I throw 90 percent of them away," he said) and he had broken them down into a conceptual hierarchy. The top level of the hierarchy divided into HUMAN, on the one hand, and NATURE on the other; and then the breakdown under HUMAN began as follows:

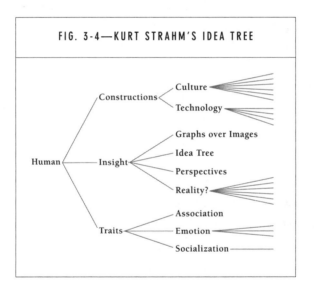

FIG. 3-4—KURT STRAHM'S IDEA TREE

"I tried to break down what I was interested in," Strahm said as he scrolled through. "It's silly, but that's the kind of person I am." Many of these ideas described art projects that Strahm felt were too grandiose for him ever to implement. For example, he pointed out one called "Car Alarm Coffin." He explained: "I hate fucking car alarms. You know this guy Issa, Darrell Issa? He's a right-wing congressman from California; he claims to have invented the car alarm. So I was going to, you know, bury him"—a rendering of Issa, that is—"in this coffin surrounded by, like, sixty car alarms, and let him have it for eternity."

Another idea was called "Accidental Street Sculpture"—he had it filed under HUMAN - CONSTRUCTIONS - TECHNOLOGY - JUNK—and had a single picture to go along with it. The idea ran as follows: "A series of snapshots of twisted street sign poles, accidental sculpture." He had taken the single picture so that, through his blog, he might explain the concept to others. I pointed out that unlike, perhaps, Car Alarm Coffin, Accidental Street Sculpture seemed eminently doable for an artist of his skill level.

"Given the time, I *could*," he replied wearily. "You know, walk every street in Manhattan. What a clichéd idea—every edition of the *New York Times*, every street in Manhattan. I thought of taking a picture of every long garbage pile in Manhattan, at the right time of day. . . . The trouble is, I've been trying to quit just enjoying having ideas, and communicate a little like you're supposed to when you do art or write, and explain in an interesting way why I found these ideas so pleasurable myself."

In his telling, no single one of Strahm's ideas ever merited much of his own respect. It was only when he laid out the *meta*-idea—how he was disseminating the ideas through his blog—that a softening, almost a sentimentality, crept into his voice. "I never had kids, I never wanted kids," he said. "So the question is, what do you pass along, when you, you know—what do you pass along? And what I want to pass along is—there's so much fucking ugliness—I would like to pass along what affected me about life, what I find deep, and, you know, meaningful, and interesting, and funny."

Looking at the painstakingly realized artwork on the walls—the cultural production of an earlier self—I realized that Strahm now saw the world with clear eyes; he had figured it out before the rest of us. It was a mug's game, these days, to spend months laboring over an art project, only to have it exhibited briefly in a gallery, perhaps purchased, but almost certainly soon forgotten. By contrast, a stripped-down, imperfectly realized project, or even just an *idea* for the project, can be disseminated, spread, appreciated in an instant; one can watch it spread online from mind to mind, see plaudits and criticisms spin out in real time; one can watch, indeed, its very abandonment, even as another idea has taken its place. The increase in pleasure is immense, and the chances of one's work enduring decreases only a small amount, falling down from a thousandth of a percent, perhaps, merely to zero.

WEEK TWO

In the left-wing political echo chamber, one significant date loomed during the month of August that year: August 8, when Connecticut senator Joe Lieberman was set to face his antiwar opponent, Ned Lamont, in the state's Democratic primary. The moderate Lieberman was, and remains today, the greatest symbol of the internecine fight over the direction of the Democratic Party, an ongoing argument about how confrontational in tone, if perhaps not in actual policy prescriptions, the party's leaders should be against their Republican opponents. Heading into the Contagious Festival that month I was well aware that August 8 lurked as a, or perhaps *the,* crucial inflection point in the competition: a moment when a truly on-the-news entry could appear and overwhelm all opponents just on the basis of its timeliness. This had happened before, during the Festival's first month, when—just as an apolitical entry was poised to walk away with the contest—the vice president of the United States suddenly, and with no advance warning, went on a hunting trip and shot another man in the face. Progressives erupted in a unanimous howl of pleasure, muffled at first as mock indignation but then (once it was clear that the shootee would survive) yawped with untrammeled glee. Feverishly did the Internet elves set to

work, and within days the Contagious Festival had been entirely transformed. One brand-new entry, "Quail Hunting with Dick Cheney," offered a Flash-animated game in which players tried to have a cartoon
Cheney shoot a quail; in all cases he would miss the quarry and hit
one of his hunting party instead. Another was Paul Hipp's "Cheney
Plays Folsom Prison," a parody of the Johnny Cash song in which the
narrator "shot a man in Reno just to watch him die." Both of these entries quickly swamped the totals of the previous leaders, attracting
more than a hundred thousand visitors each. It was inevitable that
August would see some Lieberman entries emerge, and in some ways
this was dangerous precisely for its being predictable. That is, wise
meme-makers *knew* that the conversation would be dominated by Lieberman for those weeks in August, because the date had been set in
advance.

The August 8 date represented what the old media call a *peg,* and
indeed awareness of pegs is just one example of the democratization of
the media mind. Media people see the world through a filter of pegs, in
part because of practical considerations: all stories take time to research, to write, to edit, to be produced or printed, and to be distributed. So both reporter and editor are forced to do mental math, asking
themselves not, Is the story interesting now?, but rather, Will the story
still be interesting after the researching, writing, editing, and printing
have all run their course? The solution is the use of pegs. If one knows
that a book by an author is to be released in a certain month, then one
can prepare a major profile of that author for that same month. If one
knows, for example, that a documentary featuring Al Gore is to emerge
in a certain week, then one can, as *New York Magazine* cannily did,
produce a cover package touting the "Al Gore boomlet" about a possible
2008 presidential run on his part. (Of course, he never showed any intention of running.)

The Lieberman primary was the perfect peg, and, as I would soon
discover, one Festival entrant had in fact played it to the hilt. Sometime

in the early hours of August 8 it arrived: "Joe & Dub's Fabulous Wedding," a Flash-animated fantasia in which Joe Lieberman and George W. Bush are wed in an elaborate ceremony, with various Republican heavies serving as attendants. It was a great viral idea not only for its peg, but for the simplicity and immediacy of its conception: just a phrase in an e-mail accompanying the link—e.g., "Bush and Lieberman get gay-married!"—would suffice to make a receptive recipient click. And sure enough, by the following day the site had pulled away to a clear lead:

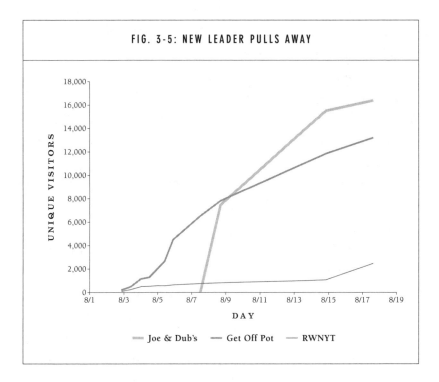

FIG. 3-5: NEW LEADER PULLS AWAY

"Joe & Dub's Fabulous Wedding" was created by Gary Lee Stewart, a fiftysomething former construction worker who lives in a leafy but rundown neighborhood on the far east side of St. Paul, Minnesota. "Is it okay if I smoke?" he asked when I went to visit him, almost as soon as I had set foot inside his apartment. "'Cause I don't ever not smoke." It was daytime but one might not have known it. Although his picture window looked out on a small park in the rear of his apartment complex, the vertical blinds were shut tight and seemed to have been kept that way for some time. Gary himself, though, was a radiant individual, with unkempt blond hair, a handlebar mustache, and a constant, almost manic, grin. His photophobic habits, he explained, were simply a byproduct of his creative schedule. "I'll go, like, forty-eight hours, even longer," he said, when in the throes of a project.

One such project was "Joe & Dub's Fabulous Wedding." The ironies surrounding its success were many. First, for an animator in Flash (which Gary called "the white trash of movies"), Gary was astonishingly unsavvy with computers. He had made the entire project using only six commands that a friend had taught him; lacking a broadband Internet connection, he couldn't even watch his own video online, nor could he view most of his competition. Second, although the entry had been accused (credibly) of homophobia, Gary was perhaps the campiest gay man I had ever met. Over his computer speakers, he played me tracks from his 1987 self-produced EP, *StereoTopically Gay Music*, which included a ribald song about the Supreme Court's 1986 anti-sodomy decision in *Bowers v. Hardwick*. "Suddenly they're on my back," he sings of the Justices, "Upholding rigid penal codes / Emptying their thick workloads / I feel deeply violated and degraded as they draw / Their far-reaching and gripping / Uncut, pulsating, and dripping / Penetrating, probing, grueling / Filthy, smelly ruling / From the tight and twitching annals of the law." (If only David Lat had started his legal blog twenty years earlier, Stewart would have been a viral sensation way back then.) Even the names of Stewart's bands were pregnant with innuendo: "Gary Lee Stewart and the ScuttleButts"; "the Saggy Bottom Girls Jug Band."

Gary lived on disability and social security. Back in 1973 he was, he claimed plausibly, the "first out gay man in Duluth"; he had been working in a government job, but lost it, he said, during one of the Nixon-era purges of gays from the civil service. After that he worked construction— "mostly remodeling, but I've done the real thing. I helped pour those silos up in Duluth, those big green towers." As one might imagine, he kept his sexual orientation to himself.

"But somebody always seemed to know, you know?" he added. "I remember a crane operator who was staring at me, and I realized that I had seen him at a gay bar in Des Moines. And he didn't like that there was somebody that had seen him. I was down in a hole, and I remember I had a feeling that he was going to kill me—and *could,* very easily. It would be just another industrial accident! I got out of that hole, and I never went back after that day. I never saw a glare like that before."

I asked Gary to show me what he was working on now. His computer desk had two different ashtrays within arm's length, and though he said he had wiped all the ash off the desk itself in preparation for my visit, I saw quite a bit of it still lurking about. He browsed around in his PC. "Okay, let's see—I'm working on one called 'Chickenhawk Bird Flu,'" he said, and pulled up an image. It was a composite of a small yellow bird wearing an army helmet, and onto the bird's head had been superimposed the face of Dick Cheney. Gary pulled up another image, this one animated in a minimalist style. In it, the veteran Washington correspondent (and Bush critic) Helen Thomas was fronting a ragtag band, and the musicians behind her were other media notables: TV hosts Keith Olbermann and Jon Stewart, plus the formerly kidnapped *Christian Science Monitor* reporter Jill Carroll.

In a third image, another animation, a woman strained to pull an elaborate cart across the screen. "That's Judith Miller, of course," Gary said, referring to the *New York Times* reporter who had done flawed reporting on Iraqi weapons of mass destruction. "And she's pulling a Karl

Rove wagon. A meat wagon." I looked closely at the cart's side, and in fact, it said:

DR. KARL ROVE'S
FOX NEWS
SNAKE OIL AND MEAT WAGON

"See, it's a meat wagon," Gary said. "You can see the meat hanging from it." I looked even more closely, and indeed I could.

KNOCKOUT

Tremors portending the quake that would upend the competition were felt first, I was surprised to learn after the fact, in the sedate seaside city of La Serena, Chile, founded in 1544 as a port link between Santiago and Lima and reputed still for its handsome sixteenth-century churches. On a hill called Colina el Pino at the city's eastern edge, in the compound of the Gemini Observatory—which maintains one of the world's most powerful telescopes at Cerro Tololo, farther up the Andean ridge—a thirty-seven-year-old American named Rob Norris was employed as a software engineer. As he told me later, at 4:38 p.m. local time (the same, in August, as Eastern time) on August 17, he took a break from remotely debugging some telescope code and to read the latest news at the Huffington Post. There he saw a link to the Right-Wing *New York Times*, and read it.

Two minutes later, Rob passed along the link in an instant message to his friend Chet Farmer, in Houston, Texas. Chet is from Hattiesburg, where he and Rob became friends in the fifth grade. Chet, too, is in the software business, working at a seven-person startup whose employees all work from home. Before Chile, Rob had lived in Austin, and the two would sometimes get together; "but with IM and the fact that he still

has an Austin phone number (via the magic of voice-over-IP phones),"
Chet remarked to me later via e-mail, "I almost have to GO to Austin
to notice he's not there." In addition to being a self-described "arts
geek" and "leftie (obviously)," Chet also is a "hobby blogger," maintain-
ing a blog entitled Miscellaneous Heathen. After receiving the link
from Rob, he posted the Right-Wing *New York Times* to his blog at 4:43
p.m. with a note reading: "Hilarious. Hat tip to Rob."

The readership of Miscellaneous Heathen is negligible, but it did
then have at least one extremely powerful reader: Chris Mohney, Chet's
college friend from the University of Alabama who was then the man-
aging editor of the New York gossip site Gawker. Rankings of the nation's blogs are notoriously inexact, but in one well-respected tally,
known as the TTLB Ecosystem, Gawker is the seventh-most-read
blog on the entire Internet. Within New York culture-industry circles,
Gawker has come to occupy roughly the same place that *Spy* magazine
did in the late 1980s: darkly comical, brutally mean, it crows over the
foibles of the city's most powerful or fashionable. Gawker's offices were
in SoHo, just a few hundred yards from the Huffington Post and six or
so blocks south of the print magazine where Will Murphy's alter ego
toiled away his days. And yet the Right-Wing *New York Times* took
a trail leading from Chile through Texas to arrive so near where it
started, on the front page of Gawker—where it was posted the next
morning, August 18—and soon thereafter at the top of the Contagious
Festival.

By the end of that day, Friday, August 18, the Right-Wing *New York
Times* had become one of those websites that was linked wherever you
looked. At its peak that morning it was receiving eight thousand visits
per hour. It had been featured on BoingBoing, posted to MetaFilter,
voted up on Reddit, bookmarked on del.icio.us. In the official rankings
its climb was steep and staggering, as this chart of just thirty hours'
traffic will attest:

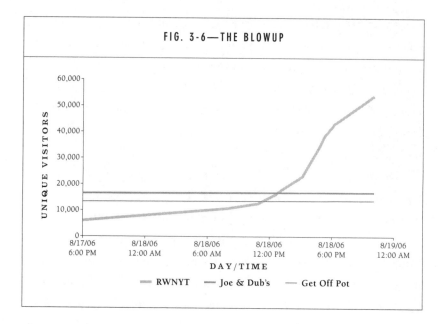

FIG. 3-6—THE BLOWUP

On surveying the rise in retrospect, I concluded that my strategy—to succeed by playing to multiple audiences—had worked. In the first and most core group, represented by the leftist blogosphere, citations of the site tended to be brief and without comment; to them the condemnation of the right implied in the parody spoke for itself. In the second, breakout group—the ironists—fans tended to cite specific, anarchic B jokes. Gawker reproduced two of the parody *Times*'s image boxes (depicting the pornographic art show called "Two Dudes Strokin' It" and the dining piece called "Cooking with Placentas and Cocaine"). On the blog of Seattle's alternative weekly *The Stranger*, editor Dan Savage made "Two Dudes Strokin' It" the title of his post. The MetaFilter poster, who calls himself "brain_drain" (in fact "a litigation attorney at a large law firm in New York City," he told me in an e-mail, though beyond that he asked to remain anonymous), took as the name of his post the title of one of the op-ed articles supposedly written by Michael Moore: "I Hate America Even More This Week." Among the third, more speculative audience—conservatives—the site's reception was not entirely warm, but nevertheless seemed as good as could be expected. David Frum, the man who as speechwriter for George W. Bush invented the phrase "axis of evil," linked to it in his blog on the *National Review* website, driving a considerable amount of traffic. At the site Hot Air, a poster named AllahPundit gave it a glowing review, and cited one of the parody's specifically conservative jokes—"Vows: Jane Fonda, 69, and Ayman al-Zawahiri, 55"—adding, "It's that good."

POSTGAME

After that weekend, the contest was essentially over, even though two entire weeks of it remained. The Right-Wing *New York Times* would finish with roughly 155,000 visitors, while no other entry made a serious move to challenge: Gary Lee Stewart and Jeff Meyers stayed in second and third place, respectively, with less than 20,000 visitors apiece:

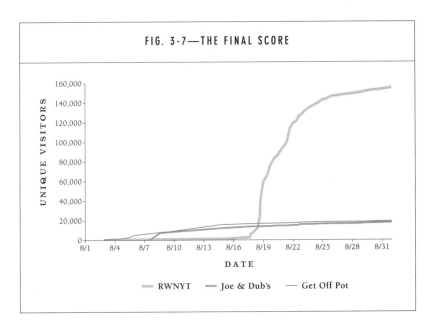

FIG. 3-7—THE FINAL SCORE

These were cumulative numbers, of course; a graph of the actual new visitors per day during the blowup looked like this:

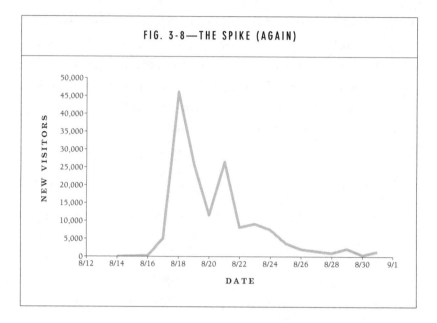

FIG. 3-8—THE SPIKE (AGAIN)

A week or so into September, I met up with Jonah for a postgame chat. I told him that Will Murphy and I would be getting a drink together near the Bowery, and he should come along. When he arrived, I said that Will was going to be late, but I bought us beers and we began to talk shop. Jonah was starting a new company of his own, called BuzzFeed, a website that would identify new trends in online conversation by crawling blogs and analyzing the links. His idea was that if the various blog posts were properly aggregated, not only would intriguing trends emerge but BuzzFeed users could read them directly in the bloggers' own words.

What was revolutionary about blogging, he pointed out, was the way that the audience could become, in effect, the actors, watching their influence on culture even as they described it. "Even just linking to something," he observed, could be an act of self-conscious trendsetting. "Marketers are telling me that *this* should be popular," as he described the blogger mentality, "but I want *this* thing to be popular, so I'm going to trumpet it myself."

I agreed. "That's one of the things that makes blogging so exciting,"

I said. "You think you're going to comment on culture, report on it by being a blogger. But in the end, you get drawn into the idea that you can *start* trends. People come in thinking they're meme-watchers, but they become meme-makers."

"Right, right," Jonah said.

"It's funny," I went on, "because as I was reporting on the Contagious Festival, there was some of that same excitement. You want to be an observer, but you get drawn into it, and you wind up wanting to be a participant."

"You mean you personally?" he asked.

"Yeah!"

"You thought to yourself, '*I can win this thing.*'"

"Right. In fact"—I paused for as much drama as I could muster—"I am Will Murphy."

"What?"

"I am Will Murphy."

"That's why he's not here yet?"

"Right."

He thought for a moment. "Now I don't feel bad that you paid for the drinks," he said. It was true: I had won $2,500, though after the two beers plus tip, it was down to $2,488.

Sitting there, it occurred to me that the two of us, Jonah and I, were part of another nascent subculture, a meta-subculture, really, which just then was slowly coalescing toward being: the *subculture of meme-makers*. They—we—might hail from different niches (comedy, art, politics, tech, publishing, etc.), but we find ourselves drawn to all online sensations, regardless of content, fascinated by how culture spreads, looking for rules and tricks to use ourselves. It was only natural that these kinds of cross-niche connections would get made; as Jonah had pointed out, memes spread precisely when they break out of their audiences and achieve a sort of transcendence of subculture, like waves so fierce they oversweep walls.

Contemplating the viral successes of amateur memetic engineers, one could see very vividly the revolution in media that Internet boosters believe to be taking place. Here were individuals casting off their individual (sub)cultural blinders in order to analyze, unsentimentally, what spreads online and how. Instead of remaining passive members of a mass-media audience, they were burrowing inside the media machine, divining the rules behind the behavior of that audience and, ultimately, themselves as media-consuming individuals. As in a flash mob, the participants had become their own show. They were wresting down the idols of the corporate cultural overlords, so as to install a glorious new order run by the many, not the few: a thousand points of buzz.

But if a subculture of meme-makers is emerging, the mentality on which it is converging is a dispiritingly familiar one: it is the mind-set of the marketer, drunk on numbers, single-mindedly obsessed with gathering attention, engineering sudden spikes. Rather than destroying the idols of mass culture, we are merely melting them down to forge a million pocket-sized replicas. Our mental transformation mirrors the shift in the corporation when, through the poll and the focus group and market research during the twentieth century, it made its crucial quantitative turn. In the twenty-first century, in the thrall of the media mind, ordinary Americans are learning how to focus-group-test themselves.

This canny awareness does create a challenge for corporations, though not at all the revolutionary threat that our apostles of people power would like to believe. As consumers have become conscious of just how they are induced to buy, companies have attempted to refine (and in some cases rethink) their own tricks of mass culture to take this awareness into account. One obvious gambit along these lines has been the snarky meta-irony of so much contemporary advertising, which unctuously winks at its own manipulative power. But more recently, in their turn to so-called viral and word-of-mouth marketing, corporations are attempting to enlist consumers as unpaid salespeople of sorts, responsible for the creation and propagation of the marketing message. Where advertising and focus groups and direct marketing, as experiments, hid the science from the subjects—leaving the consumer on the opaque side of the one-way mirror—these new word-of-mouth methods of marketing are exploring the idea that consumers can be confederates: secret agents for the corporate cause.

It is this phenomenon, its promise and its perils, that we explore in chapter 4.

4.

AGENT ZERO

EXPERIMENT:
BILL SHILLER

DESPERATION

More than three years after flash mobs were a nanostory, they became a viral marketing campaign. I first read about it in a *Financial Times* column, e-mailed to me by a friend. A "series of flash mobbing events," the *FT* reported, was "being staged by Ford Motor with Sony Pictures Digital to promote the launch of the new Ford Fusion car." The events were called "Fusion Flash Concerts." *Weren't you always concerned about this?* my friend had written in the subject heading. In fact, I had never been concerned about it but rather had expected and even welcomed it, since appropriation of the flash mob by the nation's large conglomerates would, I reasoned, be its final (and fatal) phase. Up to this point, the only sign of pilferage had been a 2004 episode of *CSI: Miami*, the nation's third-top-rated television show. Entitled "Murder in a Flash," the episode begins with a flash mob that leaves a dead body in its aftermath, but by the end—and here is where the writers really earned their residuals—we learn that the stiff had been there already, the mob sent later by an honest teen to clue police in to the deed.

But that had been a mere reference to flash mobs, whereas Fusion Flash Concerts was a true co-optation—Ford was planning to create real-life flash mobs, in order to make its product seem cool. By presenting myself as an interested member of the news media, I was able to confirm this latter point with Ford directly. Ford was, a spokesman told me by phone, "looking for cool ways to connect with their target audience," at both a "price point" and what he called a "cool point." The flash concerts idea, he said, had "a spontaneity and a cool factor that was attached to it."

He invited me to come and see the flash concert in Boston, at City Hall Plaza. The featured act would be a band called Staind, whose upcoming album *Rolling Stone* had described as "a unique combo of AA-meeting ballads and fetal-position metal." Most concertgoers would have to register at the site and wait to receive the details just beforehand, but to a reporter in good standing he was willing to reveal the secret show date. It was a week and a half away, in early August—the same date, as a matter of fact, that Staind's new album was to be released.

City Hall Plaza is a singularly poor spot to hold a flash mob. A good mob site, I would assert with some experience, must conspire to make a mob matter: it must be confined enough to make the mob seem grand, unassuming enough to make the mob seem absurd, well-trafficked enough to provide an audience for the mob's visual shock. In City Hall Plaza, by contrast, it is as if the urban space had been calibrated to render futile-seeming any gathering, large or small, attempted anywhere on its arid expanse. All the nearby buildings seem to be facing away, making the plaza's eleven acres of concrete and brick feel like the world's largest back alleyway. There is no nearby community to speak of, the historic neighborhood there—the old Scollay Square, a

convivial knot of tightly packed apartment houses and popular bur-
lesque theaters—having been entirely razed in the early 1960s. In its
stead was laid down a plaza so devoid of benches, greenery, and other
signposts of human hospitality that even on the loveliest fall weekend,
when the Common and Esplanade and other public spaces teem with
Bostonians at leisure, the plaza stands utterly empty save for the occasional skateboarder grinding a lonely path across its long, shallow steps
to nowhere. The Hall itself, hailed at its construction as a paragon of
what then was approvingly called the New Brutalist movement, ap-
proximates both the shape and the charm of an offshore oil platform;
its concrete facade is now pocked with spalls and dulled by weeping
dark patches of smut.

Wandering the site two hours before showtime, I was struck by how
every vestige of "flash" had already been stripped from the evening's
event. The "last-minute" e-mails had in fact gone out six days beforehand. Two radio stations had been tapped to promote the show with
ads ("just to pump everything up," another Ford rep had told me).
Newspapers had even listed the concert in their daily arts calendars.
Here at City Hall Plaza a tremendous soundstage had already been
erected, its prodigious backdrop displaying the cover art from Staind's
new album. Phalanxes of motorbike cops rumbled around, eyeing the
hundred-strong klatch of diehard Stainders lumped directly in front of
the empty stage. Ford had already set up a hospitality tent, had cor-
doned off a VIP area, and, atop yard-high stands in the near distance,
had perched two new Ford Fusions, the eponymous guests of honor,
tilted widthwise as if banking gnarly turns.

While we waited for the soundcheck, Barry Grant, a Ford rep, offered to show me around the product. Barry was a sunny fellow whose
face had a pleasingly Mephistophelian aspect, with a neat goatee and a
shaved head atop which unnecessary sunglasses were perched. As
Barry and I cut through the crowd toward the Fusions, I asked him in
very general terms who Ford thought the car's ideal customer was

likely to be. As it turns out, he said, the company had done a great deal of "psychographic profiling" on just this question.

"What we're looking at here is someone who's moving ahead in their lives, they're moving forward in their career," he said. "It's a person who's entrepreneurial, thinking outside the box. They're generally young, they're either in a relationship now or are getting married sometime soon, and they're into activities like music, technology, exercise."

Really, I reflected, he was describing no one so much as me, whose own marriage was then only six weeks away and who was, at least at that moment, in possession of a gym membership.*

"See the contrast stitching, and the nice chrome accents and details, the piano-black finish—all for less than twenty and a half." Barry gestured through the window at the dash. "It's all about how this vehicle looks, how it feels, how it moves, you know?" He delivered his final judgment with genuine awe: "I think we've hit on all the senses with this one."

As we talked, a roadie onstage had begun to test the drums individually. With each stroke a deafening clap shot out across the plaza, caromed off a Brutalist wall, and rebounded past us again, barely diminished. I looked around at the crowd, the average age of which was perhaps nineteen, a motley collection of wan goth girls, leathery semi-drifters, wiry North Shore bullies in wife-beaters. A bleached blonde wandered by in a tight T-shirt reading NO BAR'S TOO FAR. I remarked to Barry that psychographically speaking, the crowd did not seem to be what he and Ford had in mind.

It was true, Barry acknowledged, that the Fusion was "really going for people who are midtwenties to, say, late thirties," but he added: "We know the vehicle has youth appeal. . . . This vehicle, it kind of shakes things up a little bit. I mean, look at the black one—I think it looks a little bit different from an Accord or Camry," he said, his tone implying

---

* Since canceled.

severe understatement. I looked at the black one. In point of fact, the vehicle shook nothing up. Its design was supremely generic, as if an Accord, a Camry, and every other sedan on the market had been meticulously averaged together.

The soundcheck finally went on at nearly six thirty, and afterward I returned to the media desk to wait for the show. A giant Ford rep with a graying goatee asked me about my story. I was writing about what happened to flash mobs, I told him.

He looked at me intensely. "They're dead," I heard him say. I stared back at him.

"The Dead," he said again. "They'd do concerts like this. And raves. Flash concerts are pretty much like raves." I could barely hide my disappointment at this turn. We looked out at the restless crowd of "flash mobbers" packing up against the stage, their boredom having prompted them to throw a hailstorm of increasingly dangerous material into the air: balloons, then empty water bottles, then full water bottles, then aluminum cans. Sporadic fistfights had begun to break out.

The Ford rep shook his head at the scene and smiled. "Everybody wants to feel like an insider," he said.

"WORD-OF-MOUTH" MARKETING

If there has been a single most important trend in marketing during the first decade of the twenty-first century, it has been corporate America's slavering over viral culture, its hunger to create and own just the sort of contagious explosions that flash mobs represented. For the marketers who want to colonize this culture, there is now even a trade organization, called the Word of Mouth Marketing Association (WOMMA)— "word of mouth," aka WOM, having emerged as the favored term of art to encompass not just viral ads but the larger goal of insinuating corporate messages into private conversations. The extent of the appetite was on display one sunny December in Washington, D.C., where a few hundred professional word-of-mouth practitioners gathered for WOMMA's annual meeting, held at a convention hall called the Ronald Reagan Building.

Word-of-mouth marketing is a response to a problem that, at the convention, was laid out succinctly in a slide by Peter Kim, an analyst for Forrester Research. It is a problem with conventional advertising, which no longer works the way it once did. In just the four years between 2002 and 2006, based on Forrester surveys, the percentage of Americans who said that "Ads are a good way to learn about products" had dropped more than twenty-five points, from 78 percent to 52 percent. Similar drops were evident in how many Americans said they "buy because of ads," or said that "companies tell the truth in ads." It is partly a problem of dwindling attention, and rising clutter—as marketing guru Seth Godin points out in his book *Permission Marketing*, a single visit to a supermarket entails suffering through a barrage of ten thousand advertising messages. It is also a problem of increased sophistication, of consumers having internalized the visual and rhetorical tricks of advertising and having learned to tune them out.

But behind this dark problem twinkled the rays of opportunity. The good news was delivered by Ed Keller, the president of WOMMA's board of directors, and Brad Fay, whose firm, Keller Fay, does sophisticated tracking of consumers' conversations. In a program called TalkTrack™, the firm had recruited almost four thousand consumers to record twenty-four-hour diaries of all their conversations, both online and offline. The consumers made notes in these diaries whenever "marketing-relevant" topics came up—from within sixteen sectors ranging from dining and beverages to health care and public affairs—and, better yet, whenever specific brands were mentioned. The results were tantalizing to the crowd, and over the following days at the conference I heard them cited over and over again, in particular these two, simplest statistics:

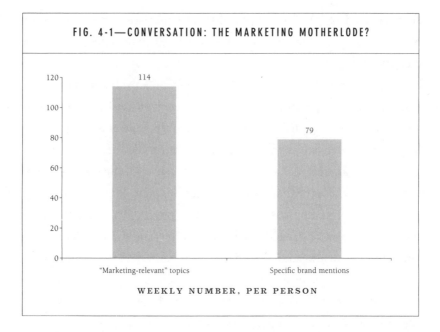

FIG. 4-1—CONVERSATION: THE MARKETING MOTHERLODE?

WEEKLY NUMBER, PER PERSON

What makes these conversational mentions so enticing is that unlike ads, consumers seem to act on them: Messrs. Keller and Fay found that in more than three-quarters of instances, the receiver of a brand mention deemed the information to be "highly credible" or "fairly credible," and in nearly as many cases—65 percent—the recipients said they were "highly likely" or "somewhat likely" to buy based on the information.

Thus quantified, the personal conversations of average Americans suddenly stood glimmering before the assembled marketers like empty billboards, waiting to be emblazoned for corporate gain. Conversations were the new advertising frontier, and the conference's small-group presentations all concerned themselves with how to rush in and stake a claim. The simplest approach was video ads, made just like television spots but intended purely to go viral online. But almost everyone wanted to go even further. A number of intrepid companies, including Pepsi, Jeep, Sprint, and Heinz Ketchup, had launched programs by which consumers could make their *own* ads, so much did they presumably love the brands in question. More common were special sites with branded entertainment, designed to draw consumers into a "relationship," no matter how mundane the product. Kraft Foods made an elaborate site for "St. Arvin" University (*starvin'*—get it?) with college-themed videos. Hanes Socks created an animated online poker game where one's opponents were sock puppets. I Can't Believe It's Not Butter launched an incredibly elaborate site that included guest voices by Fabio and an appallingly terrible animated soap opera with a butter-substitute theme.

Ford, as it happens, had gotten into this particular act too; at the time of the conference it was running an elaborate website called Ford Bold Moves, which described itself as follows: "Ford Bold Moves is a video documentary series that takes you inside Ford Motor Company as it attempts one of the largest corporate turnarounds in history. . . . Bold Moves also involves you in the actual corporate decision-making process—allowing you to engage, debate and discuss what you think is relevant." What the consumers found irrelevant, it seems, was Ford Bold Moves in its entirety: the number of blog posts linking to Ford Bold Moves during the entire six months of its operation was eight. It was hard to imagine that the number of consumers seeking out a soap opera about I Can't Believe It's Not Butter was significantly greater than that. Generally I am not disposed to pitying corporations, but I confess that sitting there in the Ronald Reagan Building, I found something almost heartbreaking about most of these WOM campaigns, with their grandiose expectations of how deeply consumers want a "relationship" with the companies that manufacture and sell them stuff.

I thought about Ford during its mid-1980s revival, when my parents, who like most other Americans then had just about given up on Detroit and its hulking, unreliable cars, were won over by the Ford Taurus. The 1986 Taurus ads can be found on YouTube, and what seems remarkable about them today (besides the embarrassing hairdos and music) is how actively they sell the product—how much they assume that the person on the other side of the screen is not some puppyish potential brand evangelist but someone for whom a product was to serve a specific purpose in an otherwise nonbranded life. We see parents and kids packing up their Taurus sedan. "The traditional vacation in the family car," the announcer intones. "Except one thing's changed— *the family car.*" Ka-pow! Key change, and the singing starts: *"Taur-us!"* We see a montage of all the great features of the Taurus, from its curvy design to its innovative, computerized-looking dashboard, which made driving a Taurus in 1986 feel like flying a spaceship. And then here comes the singing again:

> *Now, there's an American car—*
> *That has exactly what—*
> *We've been looking for—Taur-us!*

The ad ends with the Ford corporate jingle of the day: "Have you driven a Ford lately?" This jingle, the reader may recall, was delivered in a singsong cadence, a perfect pause interposed between "Ford" and "lately"—the joke being that of course you'd driven a Ford before, but it was back when Fords were no good, or *even further* back when they were good; but today they were *good again,* and if you hadn't driven one lately then wow, you should.

The jingle represented an era when advertising was *active,* but now the jingle is dead, replaced by licensed pop songs or by generic pop songs designed to sound like whatever is on the radio at that moment. Today, advertisers seem to think that their best strategy is to be *reactive,* giving us whatever "brand experience" we want right now, allowing us to "hijack" their brands, in return for what they hope will be a lasting sort of engagement, even devotion. It is, I fear, a leap of faith from which they are unlikely to emerge uninjured.

EXPERIMENT: BILL SHILLER

One has to marvel at what these corporations imagine their customer today to be: an impossibly enthusiastic creature who loves their brands so much that he wants not merely to buy their products, and even on some level to *identify* with them, but moreover wants to spend a not insignificant portion of his leisure time self-consciously working as an *evangelist* for them, as if he were a traveling salesman, except without the pay or the ready opportunities for adultery. It occurred to me that I should try to *be* this customer, at least for a short while, in order better to understand this odd proposed marriage between hawker and sucker. When a consumer becomes a de facto salesperson, is he or she still a consumer in the same way? How does his relationship with the product change? Is she still *being sold* on the product or is she now, on some level, *selling herself* on it?

Hence the birth of Bill Shiller, the ideal viral consumer, a man who behaves exactly as his corporate interlocutors desire him to do. He was born with a minimum of labor: I simply set him up a Gmail account (bill.shiller@gmail.com) and a MySpace page (www.myspace.com/bill shiller) and immediately began to cultivate proactive relationships with brands.* Every company today seems to think that its customers want them to provide entertainment, or even "community," and as Bill Shiller I endeavored to prove them correct. I joined "Weber Nation," a virtual realm where owners of Weber Grills can share stories about how much they love them. I enlisted in the "Pontiac Underground," a message board "where passion for Pontiac is driven by you." I signed up for the "Diesel Cult," for devotees of Diesel jeans. ("Fill out

---

* Facebook, which has so far been more successful than MySpace in restraining corporate marketing, had not yet emerged as the dominant social-networking site.

this form and hopefully you will be accepted," the signup page said. I did—and I was!) I set up an account with MyCokeRewards.com, making sure to leave checked the boxes inviting promotional e-mails not just from Coke but their countless "partners": Kodak, Adidas, Six Flags, Blockbuster, Delta. I lounged around for a bit in Pepsi World, playing animated games (in one, an Eskimo child catches snowflakes on his tongue as Pepsi cans periodically pop out of the snow behind him) and designing my own pimped-out automobile rims. On a similarly urban tip, I layered up some hip-hop beats using the Verizon Beatbox Mixer. I strolled through Want2bSquare.com, a strangely abstract virtual world created to promote the Toyota Scion. I created a page at Krystal Lovers, an inexplicable MySpace–style social networking site created by the Southern fast-food chain.

One might imagine that the typical consumer, with a hundred cable channels, YouTube, and BitTorrent downloads at his disposal, is unlikely to spend much time on corporate websites watching videos about their products. But the designers of word-of-mouth marketing campaigns do not see it this way, and Bill Shiller did not either. I turned on Bud.tv, the beer giant's online television network, featuring advertisements and "shows" that feel like advertisements. At an Intel site called ObsoletePC.org, I watched user-generated-looking videos (real? staged?) in which people come up with zany new uses for their old computers. I sat through the first "webisode" on "In the Motherhood," an unfathomably bad comedy series "conceived" by the unholy union of Suave, the haircare-products company, and Sprint, the telecommunications provider. I surfed through Kleenex's LetItOut.com, to which users are supposed to contribute tear-jerking videos, photos, and aphorisms. At MyCadillacStory.com, I viewed photos and testimonials from Cadillac enthusiasts, people like Ian Nelson, who wrote: "You see, I am not only a Cadillac fan, but a fan of an art form that I feel too many overlook today: PURE unadulterated American luxury."

On MySpace, Bill Shiller sought out corporations as his only companions. A minimalist cartoon square named "Smart" was the avatar of Wendy's fast-food chain. "It takes flare to be a square to be hard core enough to dare to be made the way you like, to be JUICY to be FRESH to be BEEFY is to be the best," its profile said. I asked the square to be my friend, and was pleased when it accepted. Sprite's profile was called Sublymonal; "I am a combination of lemon and lime. I am refreshing. Be my friend," it said, and Bill Shiller complied. MAKE FRIENDS WITH AQUA-FINA® AND MAKE YOUR BODY HAPPY®! said Aquafina's profile, and this I did too. Coke, for its part, had a profile called Virtual Thirst: twenty-three years old, female, in Atlanta, Georgia, with a zodiac sign of Aries. She had only 159 friends; Dell Computer, meanwhile, had more than 8,000 friends, and some of them had left testimonials, e.g.: "dell laptop fan, just stoppin in . . . showing some luv . . . if thats possible." Another: "happy halloween!" Even the Ford Fusion had a page; status: "Swinger."

After two days, I had twenty-eight friends: three fast-food chains, three cell-phone companies, six cars, six beverages, three network television shows, one Hollywood movie, and two video-game consoles, plus Dell, Nike, Starbucks, and an acne cream. I sent all of these friends a bulletin. It read:

> Sorry I haven't had a chance to write each of you individually. But I want you to know that I love all of you. Friends are people (or entities) who help each other out, and I'm there for you whenever you need me. Love, Bill Shiller.

PAYDIRT

The Viral Factory, an all-viral ad agency started in London in 2000, keeps its U.S. headquarters in a low-slung redbrick building on a lazy block in Santa Monica, California. The firm shares its building with other, more traditional advertising firms, but its own offices are in a back room, a garagelike space with an oddly arced ceiling, cinderblock walls, and a concrete floor across which a fleet of mismatched tables are erratically deployed. Lying on one of them, the day I visited, was a gorilla mask of medium verisimilitude: not a drugstore item, but far from Hollywood-grade either—the caliber of gorilla mask whose wearing connotes an expensive sort of irony. It was a prop, said Henry Cowling, head of the Viral Factory's U.S. office, from a recent shoot for IBM.

Unsurprisingly, a firm whose ads are exclusively viral makes such ads exceptionally well. As Cowling walked me through a show reel of the firm's work, I was shocked at how many of the ads I had already seen, whether in e-mails or on blogs: ads for MTV, Trojan condoms, and even Ford. The Ford ad was from 2004, and I recalled it quite vividly from when I had seen it back then. A small Ford sedan sits parked on a quiet, leafy street, while in the foreground a pigeon malingers in a tree. After a long pause, the pigeon flies down toward the car; but just as it alights, the hood pops up to clout it, knocking the pigeon into the street to its apparent demise. As I recalled, its spread had seemed driven largely, if not entirely, by disbelief that Ford could have created an ad so cruel.

When I brought up this controversy, Cowling beamed—this had been entirely the point. "The fact that it was a pigeon, and the fact that pigeons crap on cars—it polarizes people," he said. Cowling, twenty-seven, is tall, gregarious, and lanky, with curly red hair and a thick London accent; this day he wore a brown knit cap and a long-sleeved black T-shirt. "On the one hand, you got people who say, quite rightly, 'We shouldn't advocate cruelty to animals.' And on the other hand, 'That pigeon shat all over my fucking car,' excuse my language. There is a debate; there is an argument. And where you have an argument, you have people talking. And where you have people talking, you have people posting and people sending stuff around and [*pop!*]"—here he snapped his fingers—"that's *paydirt*."

Having read all the chatter online about the ad myself, though, I was sure that buying a Ford had been the last thing on the minds of anyone—even the ad's defenders. The problem with this spot was similar, really, to the problem with the Fusion Flash Concert: Ford had given itself a mandate to seem youthful, edgy, anarchic, despite the fact that its cars' virtues were simply not these. Cowling showed me another viral video, this one made for Remington, the staid British maker of electric shavers. Shot in faux-documentary style, and purporting to promote the "spring/summer collection" of a stylist named Stefane Monzön, the video opens with testimonials from top models about Monzön's abilities. As the video goes along, we slowly come to realize that what Monzön is a stylist of is in fact the models' pubic hair, and the reel ends with a bona fide catwalk show of naked models with flamboyantly coiffed pudenda. It's a truly jaw-dropping ad, and I was not surprised to see the chart of its viewership in its first twelve weeks, another prodigious spike:

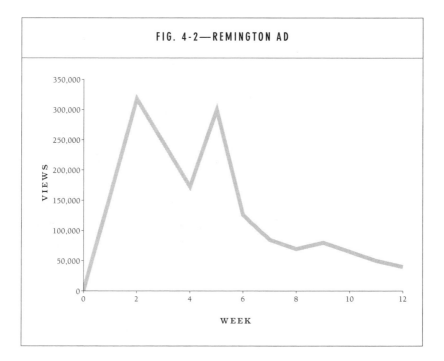

FIG. 4-2—REMINGTON AD

But I also had to wonder how much benefit to Remington this ad really generated. Viral advertising seemed like it could only push the meaning of a brand in one direction: down. That is, more irreverent, more juvenile, more poking fun at itself—what Cowling called "self-reflective," by which he meant "acknowledging that a brand is not necessarily bulletproof." All to the good, perhaps, for many products with an inherently viral appeal—video games, rock bands, movies like *The Blair Witch Project*. But what of the business that hoped to sell its products on the basis of reliability, trust, longevity? Remington and Ford had given me something to laugh at, but did I want to laugh when buying a shaver or, God help me, a car? Viral advertising seemed like a Hail Mary pass to sell to my generation and the ones after mine, and its basic premise seemed to be that adult products needed to be sold as if to adolescents.

I gave Cowling the example of the organic grocery chain Whole Foods, a brand I instinctively loathed in part because as a young married, I knew it was the kind of company that expected soon to have its talons in me. Whole Foods had not, to my knowledge, unleashed a viral marketing campaign, at least not yet. How, I asked Cowling, could a company like Whole Foods go "viral" but still convey the basic solidity, even stolidity, that was its primary selling point? Cowling turned the question over in his mind as he talked. "The whole point about social networking online is sharing your identity with people. Your identity as a consumer; your identity as an *entertainment* consumer," he said. "Advocating something from Whole Foods is saying something about yourself, so there is a motivator for someone to pass [an ad] on." Sensibly, Cowling ruled out the cruelty-to-animals route—"Obviously we couldn't make something like the Ford SportKa viral for Whole Foods; it just doesn't seem like a fit." But, as he noted, the Whole Foods brand was wrapped up in a "conversation" about organic food, conservation, the environment. And this, he wisely noted, was "a polarizing conversation. It's something that can create discussion—perhaps an argument.

And like I said, when you have discussion, you have viral. In a lot of ways, Whole Foods would be a really, really good match for a viral campaign, just because it's a brand that taps into that broader meta-conversation, as it were."

There was another element to the pigeon spot that we hadn't discussed yet: a controversy, intentional or no, as to whether the ad had actually been made by Ford. Ambiguity on these matters seemed to have become a common feature of online advertising. Just a few months beforehand, WOMMA had disciplined Edelman, a PR agency, for its having created two fake blogs on behalf of Wal-Mart—one, ironically enough, was called Paidcritics.com, its name referring not its own paid authors but to the "paid critics" who attack Wal-Mart. With viral video ads, pains are frequently taken to misdirect viewers about who is behind an ad or how it was disseminated. Certainly it was true of the Viral Factory's ads: in a few cases I had seen them without realizing they were intended as ads for anything at all. In one ad for Hewlett-Packard, a home-movie-style video, an anonymous office worker shows off his astonishing finger skills: with his index and middle fingers he kicks around a tiny (computer-generated, it turns out) ball of crumpled yellow paper, pantomiming a soccer player on the field. Only in the background can one see the HP products—a laptop, a printer—placed strategically throughout the shots; also, at the ad's end, a URL directs viewers to a branded site called FingerSkilz.tv. It was a special effect pretending to be real, and a corporate ad pretending to be user-generated.

Cowling pointed out that just such ambiguities can help to spread a viral ad. "You think it's user-generated. Is it real? Is it not real?" he said. "You're looking for an answer somewhere, so you pass it on to someone and you get a conversation going with them."

But what about the ethical implications? "I don't believe in deceiving people," he said. "It's a question that we do get asked quite a lot: Aren't you trying to pull the wool over people's eyes? Are you duping people into partaking in this advertising campaign? The answer to that is: we make entertaining, branded content. It's generally pretty obvious that it's branded." He added: "And if it's not obvious, then it's innocuous, you know what I mean?"

CORPORATE AGENTS

Among the marquee metaphors of the new marketing paradigm, just behind illness ("viral") and apiology ("buzz") are secrecy, exclusivity, covertness—hence "guerrilla marketing," the Pontiac Underground, the Diesel Cult, the "field teams" of "agents" or "brand insiders." There are now whole networks of consumers recruited to do unpaid marketing work, and remarkably these have drawn crowds of willing participants. Perhaps the best known, BzzAgent, has more than 400,000 members who have agreed to talk about products with their friends and then write detailed "BzzReports" enumerating their chats; a group called Streetwise, which focuses on urban teens and twentysomethings, boasts 70,000, whose pro-product activities range from rating songs and movie previews to stickering city streets on behalf of corporate blockbusters; the site Tremor, created by Procter & Gamble for teen buzzmaking, has signed up 250,000 youngsters to market things to their friends and one another. All of these networks strive, in their language, to foster a sense of exclusivity: to be an "agent," a member of "the Crew."

It was exactly this sense of secret agentry that was the flash mob's greatest appeal. At least as thrilling as the fleeting events themselves were the buildups in the bars beforehand, as the mobbers milled around eyeing one another, waiting for the instructions, fully aware that they were there for the same devious purpose and yet nevertheless pretending, out of obedience toward the mob rules, not to realize this fact. Insiderness seemed to be its own reward—a lesson that has been learned by BzzAgent, too. In his book *Grapevine,* BzzAgent founder Dave Balter described the great deal of thought the company put into its rewards program, where agents received points they could redeem for free items—only to find that literally three out of four agents never redeemed their points at all. When Balter surveyed agents as to why this was, he got back creepy responses like this: "It's cool to get involved with thousands of other people around the country." "I like to be the first to know about things."

What is it about being an insider, a guerrilla, an agent, that possesses such intrinsic allure? In the mid-1970s, with the revelations of Watergate plumbery still in the air, concerned social scientists ran some experiments that demonstrated the appeal. In one, researchers at Carleton University in Canada had undergraduate subjects conduct clandestine surveillance of people supposedly chosen at random (but who in fact were confederates of the researchers). For fifteen minutes, each subject tailed a target who would sit in a chair fidgeting, then get up and wend her way through university tunnels to the library, then take a book from the shelves, then get inexplicably teary and wipe her eyes. Afterward the subjects were given a list of emotional adjectives and asked to rate, from 1 to 7, how much of each emotion the experiment had made them feel; and although the subjects' "aversion index"— which researchers derived from how "nervous" or "guilty" the exercise had made them feel—rose from a normal state to 2.61, the subjects' "thrill index" ("fun," "involving," "exciting") spiked to 5.30.

In another, even more ambitious study, a team of researchers at Florida State created a fake conspiracy to burglarize a local advertising firm and then enticed students to take part. Over dinner at a local eatery, the experimenter would open his briefcase to the student and reveal elaborate plans, including "aerial photographs of the building and the surrounding area, lists of city and state patrol cars, their routes and times, and blueprints of the advertising office." The experimenter said the heist was at the behest of the IRS, to which (he claimed) the firm owed a considerable sum of money. Nine of twenty students agreed to participate—an admirably high rate for any collegiate extracurricular activity, one imagines. (Interestingly, an alternate plot in which the IRS was not invoked, but the students were promised $2,000 for their role, drew only four of twenty subjects to agree—further confirmation of BzzAgent's discovery that thrill, rather than reward, is the salient factor.)

What the lure of the agent role confirms, of course, is in part the constant pull of obedience, the disposition to defer to authority, a fact Stanley Milgram so ably documented in his notorious experiments. Far less known, and perhaps more interesting for our word-of-mouth spymasters, is a follow-up study to Milgram's conducted seven years later by researchers at the University of Missouri at Kansas City. Put off by Milgram's deceptive practices, Charles O'Leary, Frank Willis, and Edward Tomich recruited forty subjects to duplicate Milgram's authority experiments to the letter, except with one crucial difference: the subjects were let in on the premise. Told they would not actually be delivering shocks, the students were asked nevertheless to "behave in the same way that [you] would behave had [you] not been informed"; the subjects, that is, were *self-consciously playing roles*. And yet, startlingly enough, the results achieved were almost exactly the same:

FIG. 4-3—COMPARISON OF DISTRIBUTIONS OF MAXIMUM SHOCKS ADMINISTERED

VOLTAGE RANGE	NUMBER OF SUBJECTS STOPPING	
	Milgram	O'Leary et al.
Did Not Start	0	2
15–285	0	0
300	5	0
315–390	9	10
450	26	28

This is a similar result to that achieved by Philip Zimbardo in his Stanford Prison Experiment, where students picked to play inmates and guards began, over the course of days, to act out their parts with sometimes cruel fidelity: even when we are knowingly playing a role, we are likely to inhabit that role. So merely the act of allowing oneself to be called an "agent," whether covert or overt, of a corporate brand, may encourage us to act like one, regardless of how cheeky we take that appellation to be.

But online skullduggery hardly needs to be compelled; for the secret agent is, in a sense, the main role we play in viral culture as a whole. When we all can make media, when we can propagate culture and *see that propagation succeed,* then we inherently become undercover agents of a strange sort: actors embedded in the audience, salesmen flyering our own stoop. As we post our arguments and ideas, our films and photos and songs, then count our hits as they pile up, we are gathering hard intelligence on our audience and, ultimately, on ourselves.

THE AGE OF THE MODEL

In 2000, a bestselling book came along to initiate average Americans into the mysteries of the meme. The book was entitled *The Tipping Point*, and across disparate contexts ranging from crime to education to fashion and fads it laid out the precepts of what its author, Malcolm Gladwell, called "social epidemics." The extent to which this book has captivated the American audience can hardly be overstated: it has stood for almost the entire decade among the nation's top-ten bestselling books, on first the hardback and then the paperback list, where as of this writing it remains. Gladwell is a lively and lucid writer, to be sure, but even his prodigious talent cannot account entirely for *The Tipping Point*'s peculiarly boundless success. The book tapped something latent in the culture, and any attempt to understand this decade will need to reckon with just what that something was.

Has a number-one book ever before been built on such an abstraction? A bestseller at the level achieved by *The Tipping Point* generally tells some grand American story (of a long-dead president or a particularly Great generation), sells some concrete how-to (make a million dollars, keep your man, find spiritual peace), or plumbs the life insights of its famous author, whether a movie star, a famous CEO, or the Dalai Lama. *The Tipping Point*, to the casual book browser approaching its ideas for the first time, seems not even to have a proper *subject*, its subject matter ranging from business to culture to government and politics. What the book offers its readers is not a subject but rather a *pattern*, a series of scientifically grounded rules that can be seen to hold across a collection of disparate stories.

In fact, *The Tipping Point* offers its readers precisely the social-scientific insights that businesses, together with academic research departments, have been developing and harnessing for decades. Gladwell is the bard of business and cultural scientism, singing of its epic conquests in *The Tipping Point* and his follow-up *Blink*, as well as in his frequent contributions to *The New Yorker*, captivating readers with tales of how rule-based, how predictable, and how at times even manipulable a creature is Man. The classic Gladwell protagonist is he who has divined those rules and plied them brilliantly for gain. A bookstore owner in Mississippi knows how to turn titles into sleeper bestsellers. A genius retail consultant lays bare the secrets of how Americans shop at stores. Maverick entrepreneurs build software that predicts which songs and movies will be hits.

Since *The Tipping Point*, more books have become bestsellers on the promise of revealing hidden patterns and systems undergirding everyday life; most notable among them is *Freakonomics*, in which the University of Chicago economist Steven Levitt, with the aid of his coauthor Stephen J. Dubner, tours through the counterintuitive conclusions he has reached about many different questions—from real estate to school cheating to baby names—through the judicious use of statistical analysis. Underlying the success of *The Tipping Point* and its literary progeny is, I would argue, the advent of a new and enthusiastically social-scientific way of engaging with culture. Call it the age of *the model:* our meta-analyses of culture (tipping points, long tails, crossing chasms, ideaviruses) have come to seem more relevant and vital than the content of culture itself. We have lived with mass culture long enough, understand it well enough, to see that it is formulaic and constructed, to know that it plays upon us systematically. And so we see the real vigorish is in learning not about what is cool than about *how cool works:* we want to understand the process, abstract it out to steps and charts. What Gladwell, Levitt, et al. are selling us is the demystification of ourselves. And in a sunny inversion, these books invoke notions of mystery, of discovery, of intrigue, to describe the pinning of us to the specimen paper. Here, from *Freakonomics*, is Steven Levitt's "underlying belief":

> that the modern world, despite a surfeit of obfuscation, complication, and downright deceit, is *not* impenetrable, is *not* unknowable, and—if the right questions are asked—is even more intriguing than we think. All it takes is a new way of looking.

Gladwell, in a similar vein:

> [T]he Tipping Point is a place where the unexpected becomes expected, where radical change is more than possibility. It is—contrary to all our expectations—a certainty.

These books are able to sell manipulation as magical because they hold out to readers the hope of employing these models in their own lives—*The Tipping Point*, for example, promises to show readers how "to deliberately start and control positive epidemics of [their] own," while the goal of *Freakonomics* is vaguer but no less ambitious: "You might [after finishing the book] become more skeptical of the conventional wisdom; you may begin looking for hints as to how things aren't quite what they seem; perhaps you will seek out some trove of data and sift through it, balancing your intelligence and your intuition to arrive at a glimmering new idea." Readers are supposed to fancy themselves epidemiological entrepreneurs, or actuarial adventurers: Raiders of the Lost Spreadsheet.

For decades, cultural critics have warned against a future where giant, centralized organizations (the government, or huge corporations) learn how to ply the predictability of humankind to create an effectively totalitarian society: it is such fears that have given rise to the popular (indeed, overused) adjective "Orwellian," after George Orwell, the author of *1984*. In this decade's viral culture, by contrast, we find ourselves in a similar and yet entirely different situation, where individual consumers are learning and refining the tricks of manipulation for themselves—where they serve as secret agents inside their own crowds, totaling up mentions and page views, sifting through their troves of data in a scurrilous search for gold. A parallel adjective comes readily to mind, and the finer points of the comparison might best be summarized in a table:

FIG. 4-4—ORWELLIAN VS. GLADWELLIAN

ORWELLIAN DYSTOPIA	GLADWELLIAN DYSTOPIA
Human behavior can be predicted and therefore managed, with chilling results.	Human behavior can be predicted and therefore managed—with *fascinating* results.
Mass psychology used to control millions of people.	Millions of people buy books about how to use mass psychology.
Big Brother is watching you.	Big Brother is you.

BILL SHILLER GIVES BACK

Bill Shiller, I reflected, had been greedy—he had only *taken* from the corporations, playing their online games, watching their "branded content," accepting their wisdom and recipe tips and even, on MySpace, their friendship. But what had he given back? Nothing; and in the last phase of the experiment I decided it should be incumbent upon Bill Shiller to shoulder his share. I signed up for BzzAgent, Streetwise, and (fibbing about my age a bit) even Tremor, which sent me this e-mail back: "Hey Bill, we're pumped to have you as part of the Crew. Now you get to tell everyone what you really think about the latest music, games, movies, products, and a whole lot more." It added: "Your friends will be glad you did."

As a new BzzAgent, I joined a campaign on behalf of a forthcoming line of Ziploc bags called Zip 'n Steam, which one could use to steam fresh vegetables in the microwave. A week or so after joining the Ziploc campaign, I got my Zip 'n Steam bags in the mail, as well as an e-mail from BzzAgent Jono, aka Jon O'Toole, the BzzAgent communications director who serves as the nominal head of all campaigns. BzzAgent Jono, I was told on signing up, "now uses the Ziploc® Brand Zip 'n Steam™ Bags to cook just about everything he eats—especially fresh veggies!" In Jono's own e-mail to me, he was a bit more insistent. "Are you planning on attending a cookout for the July 4th holiday?" he wrote. "Holiday events are a great place to Bzz about the bags. You can even show everyone how well the bags work by doing a demonstration and sharing the delicious results." As it happened, I *had* been invited to a Fourth of July cookout, though "cookout" was perhaps too strong a word: it was a party, really, but the hosts planned to grill on the fire escape. Later, if attendees crammed out onto the same fire escape and craned their necks just so, they would be able to see some fireworks.

At the party that evening, a drizzly Wednesday, perhaps twenty or so people were waiting for the first burgers to finish when Agent Bill

Shiller made his move. Ever since a somewhat unflattering story in the *New York Times* in 2005, BzzAgent has been very diligent with its disclosure requirements, insisting that all agents explicitly identify themselves as such whenever they are "Bzzing" about a product. In keeping with this credo, I explained the whole program to all those loitering near the microwave as I filled the Zip 'n Steam bags with asparagus and broccoli rabe. I added some sliced garlic, sealed them, and let the microwave do its magic. As promised, the bags ballooned out but did not burst. "No water is required," I said, to general nods. "The vegetables steam *in their own moisture.*"

After letting the bags cool, we all tentatively reached in, extracted some stalks, and ate them. They were a tad oversteamed but generally tasty. "Honey, come and try some viral-marketing broccoli rabe," one woman called out to her boyfriend.

"Is it reusable, the plastic bag?" asked my friend John, a BBC producer stationed in New York. I told him that it was.

This seemed to trouble Christian, a bachelor colleague of mine. "If you used the bag to cook cheese," he asked, "would the bag then retain the odor of the cheese?"

"You don't steam cheese," I pointed out.

"I've heard that plastic shouldn't be reused," interjected John's girlfriend Nomi, a graphic designer. "That more than one use of it, even if you refill a water bottle, that it starts to degrade and let bad material into what you're drinking or eating." She paused. "But obviously Ziploc didn't tell me that. A yoga teacher did."

Here was another chance to emphasize my disclosure. "From Ziploc's point of view," I pointed out, "they probably hope you don't reuse them either. Because then you'd buy more. Like me, your yoga teacher may have been hired by Ziploc as a plant."

"Well, I basically consider my yoga teacher a plant," Nomi replied. "Just in that she's a ridiculous person."

I filed my report as instructed, noting the length of my Bzz (thirty minutes) and the number of people I Bzzed to (ten). I included all of my friends' comments, including Nomi's suspicious yoga teacher. "Do you know if a program like that exists," I asked, "for marketing the bags through yoga teachers and reverse psychology?" The question went unanswered. I was, however, granted 35 BzzPoints, plus (I was pleased to note) 5 "Quality Credits" with which to help improve my "agent tier."

Meanwhile, I also had joined the faithful souls at the Ground Force Network, a guerrilla marketing group for Christians whose tagline is "the Word on the streets." Formed by two marketing firms that had collaborated on selling Mel Gibson's *The Passion of the Christ* to believing audiences, Ground Force was instrumental in spreading word about the *Chronicles of Narnia* film. On one campaign—for some Bible-themed DVD series that was offering, as a prize for team members, the chance to win a trip to Israel in a contest called "The Bible Is-Reel"— I was unable to sign up without naming at least one youth group I could help them reach.

The campaign I did join was on behalf of Cali, a nineteen-year-old "R&B flavored pop" singer who, according to her Ground Force page, "refuses to be a part of the pre-fabricated, manufactured, pretty as a picture pack." Whether pre- or postfabricated, Cali clearly had good connections, and not just in the Christian entertainment world. She had been named an "Incubator Artist" on Radio Disney—a Disney-owned network aimed at teens and preteen "tweens," with more than sixty stations nationwide—and her album was being sold exclusively at Wal-Mart. On her MySpace page I listened to her music, which I can attest is "R&B flavored" in roughly the sense that grape Jolly Ranchers are grape-flavored. Her single was a dance song called "Get Up," which might sound like a genuinely R&B-flavored title until one watches the music video, in which various people "get up" by being lifted bodily into heaven.

What could I do, I wondered, to help Cali—and, in doing so, earn myself points so I could help myself to some Ground Force Network rewards? The Cali Field Agent Headquarters page laid out the tasks, and corresponding reward points, with a precision unseen in Christendom since the medieval sale of indulgences:

Online Posting: 2 Points

Email a Friend: 2 Points

Word of Mouth: 2 Points

Add Cali as Your MySpace Friend: 3 Points

Make Cali your Top Friend on MySpace: 3 Points

Use a Cali Banner [on your website or MySpace page]: 3 Points

Write a Comment on Someone's MySpace/Facebook page about Cali: 3 Points

Write an Online Review: 5 Points

Request Cali on the Radio: 10 Points

Distribute Cali Materials: 10 Points

Get Someone to Become a Member of Cali's Team: 10 Points

Get Someone to Buy Cali's CD: 20 Points

Make Public Announcement about Cali or play her CD to 1–25 people: 5 Points

Make Public Announcement about Cali or play her CD to 25–50 people: 8 Points

Make Public Announcement about Cali or play her CD to 51–100 people: 10 Points

Make Public Announcement about Cali or play her CD to 101–200 people: 15 Points

Make Public Announcement about Cali or play her CD to 201 or more people: 20 Points

Accompanying the list was an italicized warning: *Please note: We will check all reports for accuracy and reports that do not reflect actual work will not be honored when rewards are given out.* In other words, thou shalt not bear false witness about thy buzzing for Cali. Bill Shiller added Cali as a friend on MySpace (3 points), and when she accepted he made her his top friend (3 points). Moreover, in the "Who I'd Like to Meet" section of his MySpace profile, he pasted in one of the Cali image banners (3 points). I e-mailed two friends about Cali (4 points), as well as my mom (2 points). On Wal-Mart's online store I posted a review (5 points) just by turning around slightly the promotional copy Ground Force had provided. "Too many acts that desire to connect with teens and tweens seem airbrushed, ungenuine, pretty-as-a-picture, and manufactured," I wrote. "Cali's single 'Get Up' is different: it's climbing the charts because it's pop that actually tastes like real R&B."

It was a natural fit, I realized: evangelical product evangelists. I thought about the kind of person who might play Cali's CD to more than fifty people—as "chillout music" at the Wednesday youth group meeting, perhaps, or background pop for a report to the Sunday congregation about the teen mission trip to New Orleans, with the audience unaware all the while that the kid was earning ten or more sweet points in a marketing campaign. The kid would be someone embedded in a real community, one where people trusted one another precisely not to be secret agents on behalf of anything other than their own, honest taste. The person with no community to betray has nothing left to sell out.

We often forget today that a self-conscious, role-playing breed of secret agentry used to be an integral part of our culture; indeed, it once coexisted with real community. I am referring to a host of formerly iconic organizations that are now all dead or nearly so: the Masons, the Elks, the Eagles, the Moose, the Odd Fellows, the Order of the Eastern Star, and so many more. For his seminal 2000 book *Bowling Alone*, the sociologist Robert Putnam tallied up historical membership numbers for these fraternal groups up to the present day, and the declines were unsurprisingly grim. As of 1997, the Masons were down 71 percent, the Elks down 46 percent, the Odd Fellows down 94 percent to near extinction; and no doubt the numbers have continued to slide since then, as the Internet has increasingly promised us that "community" is something to be found not together but alone, online. It is easy to look at the tens of thousands of consumers who have signed up for word-of-mouth marketing programs, as "agents" or "insiders" or "evangelists" shilling for *things,* and to imagine how in an earlier time such urges to secrecy and obedience might have been more naturally, humanly, and even rewardingly channeled into a secret handshake or a solemn oath swearing eternal brotherhood in the Loyal Order of Moose.

Does word-of-mouth marketing have a future? The question is difficult to answer, because the very shift in consumer consciousness that companies are hoping to harness—our understanding of ourselves as embedded in social networks—opens us to marketing but inoculates us against it too. Just as the "meme" concept makes us think like economists, reducing *ideas* to free-market-style constructs, the very notion of a "social network" makes us think like marketers, stripping down our sense of *community,* segmenting ourselves self-consciously into niches, reducing the unknowable richness of group relationships down to barren trees of links and nodes. This is not to say that real human relationships don't flourish online: of course they do, just as real ideas can flourish there too. But they flourish *despite* our consciousness of their networked characteristics, not because of it; we no more find friendship by "friending" people than we find love by attempting, in the second grade, to be the kid who gives out the most valentines. Instead, what we learn in these moments when we amass friends and update profiles, boiling down the interpersonal to numbers and charts, is a sense of ourselves and our social circles as products on display. We hone our sense of what's hot, and among whom; we look out for tipping points, with little care as to what is tipping or whether it deserves to do so. In such a milieu, word-of-mouth marketing is destined to be both ubiquitous and useless, for when one has developed the media mind—which is, at heart, a marketing mind—one can never stop selling, but neither can one be entirely sold.

The deeper, and more vexing, question is how a populace in the thrall of the media mind can hope to govern itself. It is to this question, finally, that we turn in chapter 5.

5.

NANOPOLITICS

EXPERIMENT:
OPPODEPOT.COM

DOG DAYS

To understand American politics today, one would do well to consider the fate of Mitt Romney's late dog. An affable Irish setter, Seamus by all accounts was a beautiful creature, a loyal son of a bitch, and a friend even to cats—a picture of him obtained by the *Boston Globe* showed two white kittens rooting, no doubt disappointedly, in his underfur. Our future historians, however, will remember Seamus Romney from his short and surprising cameo during the 2008 U.S. presidential campaign, in which his master, the former governor of Massachusetts, was a well-funded but ill-fated participant. Seamus's posthumous star turn began on June 27, 2007, when the *Globe*, in the fourth part of a seven-part series about the humanoid Romney, related an anecdote about a car trip from Boston to Lake Huron, Canada, in 1983. Romney had arrived at a novel solution for Seamus's transport, namely, the affixing of a dog carrier to the roof rack of the family station wagon. After the dog, under duress en route, unleashed a stream of diarrhea down the wagon's windows, the future governor "coolly pulled off the highway and into a service station," recounted the *Globe*. "There, he borrowed a hose, washed down Seamus and the car, then hopped back onto the highway."

Within days of this revelation, Seamus Romney had transcended doghood to achieve an ephemeral media godhood. *Time*, the *Washington Post*, the *Chicago Tribune*, the Associated Press, the Cox News Service, and even the British *Guardian* all weighed in on him that same week. But the real fire under the story was lit online, fanned by a wide network of political bloggers who, at more than sixteen months until Election Day, were already obsessively covering the campaign. Care was paid to link Seamus's treatment to the failings of the current administration. "Mitt Romney will be a great Commander-in-Chief of Abu Ghraib," quipped the Washington blog Wonkette. "Mitt Romney—Compassionate Conservative?" asked the blog Divine Democrat. "Ask Seamus." Others gleefully calculated candidate Romney's decline: "Stick a Fork in Mitt Romney; He's Done," crowed Sandra Younger in San Diego.

Defenders were few, and chimed in somewhat gingerly. "Sometimes the roof is the safest place," noted right-leaning blog The Voice of Treason. Meanwhile, parodists quickly created a blog called Dogs Against Romney, sporting pictures of scared pups and their fervent testimonials. During those two weeks in the summer of 2007, one would have been forgiven for believing, *pace* Sandra Younger, that this anecdote from a road trip twenty-four years beforehand would cause the entire candidacy of Mitt Romney to jump a guardrail, tumble down a ditch, and burst into flames.

Yet looking back on the Seamus Romney story today, what is most striking is its forgettability, how indistinguishable it seems in retrospect from the idiots' parade of meaningless stories that came to define the campaign. In July 2008, on his daily "First Read" blog, MSNBC's Chuck Todd memorably dubbed it the "A.D.D. Election," as he ran down the nanostories that had flickered through the political consciousness in just one week (I have added some clarifications in italics):

> Phil Gramm's "mental" comments [*the McCain adviser had claimed the economic recession was only "mental"*], Jesse Jackson's "nut"-ty remarks [*the African American leader had said he wanted to "cut (Obama's) nuts out"*], Iran's missile tests (and that McCain "killing them" joke), FISA [*the Foreign Intelligence Surveillance Act, which Obama had backed over liberal objections*], Clinton donors not happy with Obama's debt relief efforts (and Obama briefly forgetting to mention the former rival at a joint funder), that McCain bio spot invoking the culture wars of the 1960s, the scrutiny of the candidates' economic plans, more courting Latinos, Webb off the veep list, Carly Fiorina's Viagra/birth control comment, the T. Boone Pickens energy ad launch, the RNC energy ad and the first Obama response of the general election, and, of course, we started the week with Obama announcing he was moving the last night of the Dem convention to a football stadium. Whew.

This, indeed, was how the campaign had gone for its entire two-year run. New story followed on new story, each consuming attention for a day or two and then receding into the distance. A few of these stories touched on actual, if trivial, questions of policy (would Barack Obama meet with the leaders of rogue states? does Ron Paul actually think the United States deserved 9/11?) but the vast majority involved irrelevant foibles (John Edwards's $400 haircut), slender second-order connections (Obama's dinner parties with former Weather Underground members), past peccadilloes (Fred Thompson's lobbying career), or campaign-trail gaffes (McCain saying the Iraq war had "wasted" the lives of U.S. troops). There were literally hundreds of these tiny, irrelevant narratives, stretching out over seemingly endless months. Each nanostory followed the same pattern observable in the case of Seamus Romney—the quick, breathless uptake and a slightly slower but inexorable decline into oblivion:

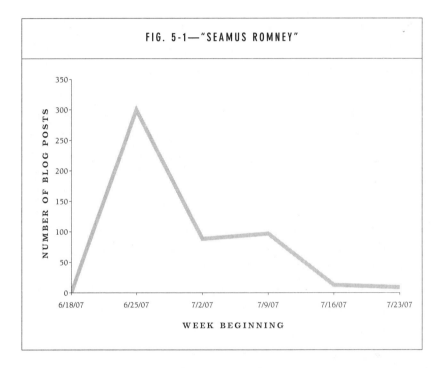

FIG. 5-1—"SEAMUS ROMNEY"

The ephemerality of our political narratives is nothing new, of course. The historian Daniel Boorstin, in his masterful 1961 book *The Image*, explored the corrosive effects of the "extravagant expectations" that TV-besotted Americans held for the world around them. Boorstin bemoaned the rise of what he called "pseudo-events," by which he meant so-called news that in fact "is not spontaneous, but comes about because someone has planned, planted, or incited it." The pseudo-event ne plus ultra is the staged PR happening—the ribbon-cutting, the press conference, the gladhand at the New Hampshire diner. But

Boorstin's broader meaning of the term was any "news" created purely to be news, from a televised debate to a government leak to a premeditated revelation in an interview.

The realm of the nanostory is a somewhat different country, founded on the revolutionary promise of our "new media": that everyone, paid and amateur alike, can be his or her own pundit. As the mass conversation has begun to move onto the Internet, where amateurs are allowed to shape it, we are beginning to learn just what happens when the narrators exponentially multiply. When our pundits are numbered not in the hundreds but in the hundreds of thousands, all of them looking not merely to parrot stories as they hear them but rather to herald new twists and turns themselves, then by necessity there are more twists, more turns, more stories told in ever shorter form.

THE MICROTREND AND THE NANOSTORY

At the peak of the Democratic primary contest, Mark Penn, pollster and chief strategist to Hillary Clinton's campaign, took time from the trail to make a public appearance at the Strand Bookstore in Manhattan. He had come to promote his book *Microtrends*, which isolated seventy-five growing demographic groups that, he argued, "are forging the shape of America and the world." In the mid-1990s, while working on Bill Clinton's reelection campaign, Penn had coined the phrase "soccer moms" to describe the cohort he predicted would decide that election; but now, he told his audience, "the era of big trends is over." For the book, he and his researchers had combed through voluminous polling data to pull out not one but scores of tiny demographic shifts. Penn's microtrends ranged from the genuinely insightful (militant illegal immigrants, women in physical blue-collar jobs) to the commonsensical (long-distance commuters, interracial families) to the frankly dubious ("shy millionaires," "aspiring snipers," and "pro-Semites"; concerning this last group, Penn writes, "Today in America, Jew-loving is a bit of a craze. Jews are in demand everywhere").

At the Strand, Penn took pains to stress that *Microtrends* was not just about politics, but given who he was, and when he was speaking, discussion naturally turned to the implications of his ideas for the current campaign. In the rise of Barack Obama, Penn saw at work the malign influence of one of his book's microtrends, a group he called "impressionable elites": upper-middle-class Americans who were so far removed from hardships that they began to care more about politicians' so-called character than about the actual issues. As reported by the *New York Observer,* one attendee responded with a skepticism that was shared by many in the audience: "Obama strikes me as a macrotrend," the man drily remarked. And indeed Obama, having just won contests in Louisiana, Maine, and Washington State, would the next day prevail in Maryland and Virginia, and a week after that in Hawaii and Wisconsin, amassing during those ten days an insurmountable advantage in delegates. Apparently, all of Penn's polling and targeting and microtrends could offer his candidate no useful insight into how to counter the broad movement at the back of her opponent, the charismatic young senator from Illinois.

I should hasten to add that this outcome did not prove Penn wrong, per se—about Obama in particular or about the "size" of trends in general. Penn's claims are essentially unprovable either way, because the very word "trend" has confusion stabbed straight through the heart of it. What Mark Penn has at his disposal, undeniably, is *data,* culled from various forays into public opinion by his own polling firm and others. What his book did was tell *stories* using that data: this survey shows one group to have increased in number, another survey shows that more Americans prefer this to that, etc. But do these stories really mean anything? Consider how they were selected: Penn and his researchers culled through polling data looking for anomalies, on the premise that unexpected results would make the most relevant microtrends. The "aspiring snipers," for example, rated among the seventy-five because one telephone poll of six hundred young Californians happened to find six who mentioned "sniper" (military, mind you) as a future goal; an intriguing result, to be sure. But a different sample on a different day would almost certainly have produced a different "microtrend"—or, more likely, none at all, because another survey in another place would have meanwhile been producing a more anomalous result. There is so much polling data being created, by Penn's firm and others, that he could assuredly rewrite his book every six months, with an entirely new crop of trends each time. The more we collect data, the more stories— micro *and* macro—we can tell about it, and the less we can expect those stories to remain valid in six months, let alone a year or a decade.

In his indispensable book *Fooled by Randomness*, the former Wall Street trader Nassim Nicholas Taleb illustrates this problem with the hypothetical case of a fortunate dentist, a man whose stock portfolio is fated to return, on average, 15 percent annually above the interest rate. The catch is that it will do so with the typical short-term volatility, i.e., his stocks will go up and down, as stocks do, even as their general march is upward. Taleb observes that if this dentist is an overly attentive man, refreshing his ticker every minute, he will open himself to great anxiety, experiencing only 241 pleasurable moments each day to 239 unpleasurable ones. Even if he checks just once a day, he will be hardly more content, experiencing perhaps sixteen good days to fourteen bad—and perhaps he will be inclined, like our business reporters do, to attribute each day's bad fortune to all manner of macro- or microtrends.* But Taleb goes on:

---

* In his later book *The Black Swan*, Taleb cites the hilarious example of two Bloomberg News headlines, issued just a half hour apart on December 15, 2003. At 1:01 p.m.: U.S. TREASURIES RISE; HUSSEIN CAPTURE MAY NOT CURB TERRORISM. At 1:31 p.m.: U.S. TREASURIES FALL; HUSSEIN CAPTURE BOOSTS ALLURE OF RISKY ASSETS.

> Consider the situation where the dentist examines his portfolio only upon receiving the monthly account from the brokerage house. As 67% of his months will be positive, he incurs only four pangs of pain per annum and eight uplifting experiences. . . . Now consider the dentist looking at his performance only every year. Over the next 20 years that he is expected to live, he will experience 19 pleasant surprises for every unpleasant one!

Taleb's point is simple: too much data leads us to see trends where none exist, to mistake randomness for order. What appear to us as microtrends, or even macrotrends, are more often than not just nanostories: narratives that the facts cannot support even into the near future. In the fable of the dentist, there is only one "trend" worth knowing—the dentist's impressive 15 percent return. But a profusion of short-term data (what Taleb calls "noise") fools him into telling himself all manner of other stories. Of course, in the era of the Internet, and the literally six-hour-long news cycle that online media (together with cable television) have engendered, too much data is the order of the day. Like the dentist, we cannot see the message for the noise. Taleb exhorts his readers to look for what he calls "Black Swans"—the sorts of singular, hard-to-predict events that (in markets, at least) tend to set off huge fundamental shifts. But in the realm of politics, one could easily argue that the opposite is true: we spend so much time looking for knockout blows, momentum swings—giant, important shifts that *might just happen this instant*—that we become blind to slow, unglamorous changes. It is the reason why one does not find many blogs (or cable-news segments) devoted to worsening income inequality, or the sorry state of the American schools, or the proliferation of nuclear weapons.

Indeed, when we do manage to focus on some crucial, fundamental story, we are often able to apprehend it only as a series of tiny, meaningless nanostories. This has been the case with global warming, an indisputably enormous problem that succeeds at staying in the popular consciousness only by way of scores of short-lived stories or controversies: cannibal polar bears, heightened hurricanes, ice-shelf collapses, the various exploits of Al Gore, etc. Even an especially hot day can occasion some well-intentioned fearmongering on the subject. The problem with this approach is that it is so easily countered by sowers of doubt. Many of the splashiest stories about global warming tend, unsurprisingly, to be those that are the most speculative or even false in their factual basis. Even the global-warming nanostories that are true can simply be rebutted with other anecdotes. Average worldwide temperature last year was lower than the previous five years. Much of Antarctica's sea ice is thickening. One could easily assemble a list of ten more such anecdotes to argue that global warming is a fiction, or at least not much of a problem. For a nation with no attention span, anecdotes are more than enough, as is evidenced by the fact that the percentage of Americans believing that humans are causing climate change has actually *declined* since 2001, from 75 percent to 71 percent. In a conversation dominated by sensational anecdotes, consensus for action is hard to arrive at. Empty controversy is far more easily had; and indeed, in a politics of nanostories, the controversy is more often than not the story. Just like Henry Cowling of the Viral Factory had put it: "When you have people talking—*paydirt.*"

THE WHOLE SHOW

This meme-warfare style of American politics was honed during the 2000 election—think of Al Gore, inventing the Internet. But it was further perfected in 2004, when Democrats, after selecting a candidate on precisely the grounds that his war-hero pedigree would render him impervious to character assassination, looked on helplessly as he fell prey to a series of attacks so damaging that the most prominent among them, the scurrilous accusation against John Kerry's war record by the Swift Boat Veterans for Truth, gave the English language a new name for the entire genre. The "swift-boating" of Kerry did not begin or end with the Swift Boat Veterans, of course; readers will remember, to pick just one example, an ad in which Kerry windsurfs from side to side, as distorted facts about his record are intoned on the audio track. For their part, the Democrats' inability to tar George W. Bush and his administration was not for lack of trying, as all the feverish digging into Halliburton or Bush's own Vietnam-era service record will attest.

In their 2006 book *The Way to Win*, veteran Washington journalists Mark Halperin and John Harris give a colorful and evocative name to this style of politics: the Freak Show. The phrase, they say, originated in a "late-night epiphany while channel-surfing" when one of them, or both together (as I prefer to imagine), was watching a cable-news show that featured "a collection of reporters and commentators from the Left and Right shouting at one another about the Monica Lewinsky scandal." Halperin and Harris use "Freak Show" to denote the entire "new arena in which politics is waged," and although they mean primarily the partisan media and the new media, they also include the mainstream media, insofar as Freak Show stories percolate thereinto. This inclusiveness seems right, as does the word "show," a characterization that captures the fundamental point: the chief appeal for the viewer is not information but rather a peculiar sort of entertainment, the monitoring of the partisan political contest in the same manner as one keeps up with one's favorite football team. The phrase "Freak Show" falls short, though, in its implication that this daily assemblage of tiny, ad hominem stories about politicians is just a wild corner of some larger and more sedate country fair. In fact, with the rise of the left-wing "netroots" (whose frequent, withering, and not unconvincing critiques of the so-called mainstream media have eroded trust in those outlets among liberals in the same way that right-wing groups did among conservatives during the 1990s), the slow fiscal decline of U.S. news-papers (which has further cut away at the clout, and indeed the self-confidence, of traditional news organizations), and the explosion of blogs and online video (which has multiplied the demand for more, and more viral, political stories at all hours of the day and night), it is no exaggeration to say that the Freak Show has become quite nearly the whole show.

If pressed to pick a single event that heralded the freaks' ascendance, I might even choose the announcement in November 2006, just as the 2008 presidential campaign was beginning, that John Harris himself—coauthor of *The Way to Win* and, as national political editor of the *Washington Post,* a comfortably ensconced Washington-media insider—was leaving the *Post* to head a start-up politics publication, which would publish on paper three days a week in D.C. proper but whose primary audience would be online. Leaving the *Post* along with Harris was Jim VandeHei, one of the paper's top politics correspondents, and together the two quickly made three equally impressive hires: Mike Allen came over from *Time,* Roger Simon from Bloomberg News, Ben Smith from the New York *Daily News.* Up until this point, although elite American political journalists had expended many words about how the web was changing political discourse, almost none of them (with the exception of Andrew Sullivan, the former *New Republic* editor who presciently threw himself into blogging in 1999) had in any way staked their careers on it. Now, five well-known writers had left their comfortable, reputable jobs for an unproven web venture, a fact that—for other journalists, at least—could be assigned one of two interpretations, equally frightening. The first was that Internet journalism, and the partisan mêlée it inevitably engendered, had gone mainstream; the second was that print journalism's economic prospects had sunk so low that there was little to lose by abandoning ship.

The new venture was eventually named *The Politico,* a fitting moniker in an era when Internet media encourages its niche audiences to style themselves as armchair insiders. Also fitting, given the ratings awareness that Internet-centric culture cannot avoid, is the fact that *The Politico* was a bet made with TV money: that of Allbritton Communications, the owner of ABC affiliates in Washington and six other cities. On a snowy day in February 2007, just weeks after the site had launched, I went to visit *The Politico*'s editors in Rosslyn, Virginia, at the offices that it shares with WJLA Channel 7. As I waited in the lobby, a harried-looking woman in a coat rushed in from the newsroom. "If you hear of anyplace that's out of toilet paper, let me know," she told the receptionist in urgent tones, just before speeding out the plate-glass doors. "We're doing that story again, about the run on local stores."

The Politico's desks sat back in a far corner of the newsroom, with a few printed vinyl banners bearing its logo hung haphazardly overhead. John Harris is in his midforties, balding, with a somewhat cherubic face and thick, blond eyebrows; the day I met him, he wore a pale-blue patterned shirt with a paisley tie in deep crimson. Jim VandeHei wore a dark brown blazer and jeans, and is younger, tall and slender, with a narrow face and short, dark boyish hair. "One of the insights Jim and I had over at the *Post*," Harris told me, "was that if you look at the most e-mailed stories, it tells you whether you're succeeding or not." He meant succeeding not just as journalists but as provokers of *conversation*. "Somebody sends that story in e-mail: 'Hey, did you read this?' 'Check this out.' 'This an interesting point.' 'This is bullshit.' Somebody is engaging with that story." And despite the web's reputation for sensationalism, the stories on the most e-mailed list were, he added, "the ones that we were most proud of. They were the ones that were the most serious, original, enterprising."

Harris and VandeHei began to ask themselves, Why aren't we doing that more often? Why, in Harris's words, "are we printing so many *boring* stories? Why are we doing so much obligatory duty coverage?" As an example of this latter, dutiful variety of story, VandeHei mentioned the classic pseudo-event: a presidential press conference. At major newspapers like the *Post*, he said, "you feel this sense of obligation to lead your newspaper the next day with a story about what Bush said at the press conference, even if he didn't say anything that was all that revelatory, and despite the fact that it's pretty damn stale: most news consumers have not only consumed it, they've digested it and moved on."

He contrasted this with a recent *Politico* story that, he noted, the *Post* did not touch, that "ten years ago would have been confined to the inside pages of *Roll Call*": the revelation that Rep. Loretta Sanchez (D., Calif.) had quit the Congressional Hispanic Caucus and alleged that its chairman, Rep. Joe Baca (D., Calif.), had called her a "whore." This story, VandeHei said, was "a perfect example of how media has changed. We put it upfront early on the webpage. Instantly it's linked to by Drudge and all the other blogs; Fox News is doing a story based on it; MSNBC is doing a story based on it; and then the next day, on *The Colbert Report*, he does twenty minutes on 'whore.' So you have just, from this perch, been able to reach significantly more people than I would have reached even at the *Washington Post*." The challenge for *The Politico*, he said, is "figuring out how to put things into that pipeline."

I asked them about judiciousness: How did they balance the reader's eagerness for these viral stories, on the one hand, against the potential damage, on the other hand, caused by advancing them? As examples, I named two pseudo-controversies: one about Nancy Pelosi's jet (a pointless tempest that month, involving a request for a larger airplane for the new speaker), and also another about Barack Obama's schooling in Indonesia (a right-wing magazine had claimed, entirely inaccurately, that Obama attended an Islamic madrassa as a child).

"We did not do anything on the Pelosi jet story," Harris said. "Jim, why not?"

"I dunno," VandeHei said, and mulled it over for a few moments. "If we don't have anything new and interesting to say on it, I don't want to say it. The *Washington Times* made that their story." I thought that he and Harris had misunderstood my question, but they had not; rather, they were acting out their unconcern for its basic premise.

"What you're describing," Harris said, finally, "is the classic *New York Times/Washington Post* dilemma. They see themselves as definers of reality, papers of record. They might think that the Pelosi plane story is bullshit, or they might think the Obama story is bullshit, and so they face this choice: Will we deign to acknowledge this with our reality-creating enterprise?"

This, Harris said, was not *The Politico*'s dilemma. "We do not have the sense of ourselves that we are out there defining reality—that we are the ones who can validate a story or not validate a story. That's a luxury for us; that's a burden for them. If there's a big uproar and we have something to say about the uproar, we will."

"We'd probably be *more* inclined to jump in," VandeHei said.

"If millions of people are talking about something," Harris said, "because of talk radio, or blogs, or what have you, you can't pretend it doesn't exist."

What they were describing was the emerging new culture of professional media, which increasingly is reinventing itself on an Internet model. It is the culture of the "most e-mailed list," which almost every newspaper maintains and consults—the *Washington Post* editors review the numbers in their daily two p.m. editorial meetings, while the *Los Angeles Times* editors get them in an e-mail every day. Today, to give readers the news they want is no longer cynical but rather is the height of idealism: what is a newspaper for, after all, if not to start *conversation*? As primary season neared, the mainstream organizations were starting up their own blogs, looking for faster-hitting stories, generating more e-mails and page views. If 2004 was the political Internet's first world war, 2008 threatened to go thermonuclear.

EXPERIMENT: OPPODEPOT.COM

After one spends enough time immersed in nanopolitics—reading blogs, listening to talk radio, watching Sunday shows—one can hardly hear the name of a candidate without the various stories about him or her flashing into one's mind. Even if one does not care *oneself* that John McCain dumped his first wife, or that Mitt Romney flip-flopped on gay rights, or Barack Obama did cocaine, or Bill Richardson is alleged to be "touchy" around women, would not these stories matter to *them,* those apostrophized millions of voters who decide the outcome? In order, therefore, to ponder the truly important questions, which are, of course, questions of *prognostication,* each reader must take an interest—purely a second-order one, mind you—in these pseudo-controversies as they carom about. Moreover, since so much of the information that fuels these controversies is already out in the public domain, one finds oneself engaging in *third*-order speculation, even, about *which* nonscandals could wind up sinking each candidate and which larger, truer storyline about these candidates they will validate. If Rudy Giuliani was vulnerable because of his complicated family history, would his candidacy be sunk by the fact that his father and uncle were convicted criminals? Or by the fact that he once was married to his first cousin? If Barack Obama was to be laid low because of his liberal extremist past, would it be his association with the Rev. Jeremiah Wright, or with the former Weatherman William Ayers, that did him in?

No longer are these sorts of meta-questions the province merely of coastal media professionals; now they are contemplated by tens or possibly hundreds of thousands of self-taught pundits and politicos across America. In one sense this is a matter of simple mathematics: in the absence of additional relevant facts, all this extra punditry must consume itself with *something.* But it is also spurred on by the media mind, the spreading awareness that anyone can act and see their actions create ripples in the wider world. Most of our new pundits are, at heart, *activists,* in a strange postspin political climate where message-making (rather than organizing) is seen as the ultimate political good. They are, to borrow a term from the previous chapter, *agents,* for whom posting a nanostory about an opponent, or drawing an argumentative line to unite three such forgettable stories, is a noble act of volunteerism.

In the early days of 2007, when some seventeen candidates were still in the running for president, I found myself unable to look away, to stop refreshing the same twenty blogs over and over again all day. I kept looking for new little stories, new tea leaves to read. Since so much of what passes for political discourse on the web is the slow meta-dismantling of one's ideological opponents, it suddenly occurred to me that Americans might value an information site that was designed to fuel this process. I felt a little of that old viral action creeping in. If thousands of Internet users could come together to create Wikipedia, a comprehensive encyclopedia to rival Britannica, then could not they also create an encyclopedia of political smears?

Such was the premise behind OppoDepot.com, "the Internet's only nonpartisan, collaborative Web 2.0 source for negative information about the 2008 presidential candidates." The name was a play on the phrase "oppo research"—short for "opposition research," the inside-Washington term for the classic political black art, the unearthing of salacious details about one's opponent. Names of political websites have gotten increasingly insidery (e.g., Talking Points Memo, *The Politico,* ABC News's The Note), and so I thought "OppoDepot" would be a catchy but properly world-weary title for the site. The idea was that each candidate would have his or her own separate page, cataloging all the decontextualized negative stories that might harm his or her candidacy. Moreover, at the bottom of each profile, a simple form would allow readers to submit any damaging factoids that weren't already present. As the site's "About Us" page explained: "We believe that to-gether, we can beat the professionals at their own game, and more quickly get the information that we need to make our important political decisions."

To start the site, I wrote (with the help of Genevieve, a researcher) a few initial "oppo" items for each candidate. In the writing, we tried to take a neutral tone, except on occasion to couch a story in terms of its political liability. E.g.:

PORN HYPOCRISY

[Sam] Brownback says he wants to crusade against pornography. But a 2005 report from Citizens for Responsibility and Ethics in Washington pointed out that Brownback gets campaign contri-butions from porn profiteers. . . .

PLAYSTATION3GATE

John Edwards likes to criticize Wal-Mart, but when he wanted a highly sought-after Sony PlayStation3 for his kids, his staff mem-bers brazenly tried to pull strings with the giant retailer. . . .

TAX HIKER

Mike Huckabee hopes to run as the right-wing darling in the GOP primaries. But if so, he'll have run away from his record, which is riddled with tax increases. . . .

Web design was graciously provided, again, by Brian, who gave OppoDepot just the right Web 2.0 sunniness: an airy white look with pastel, bubbly buttons. He also had the idea for "MyOppo," a service that would beam negative information to readers' mobile phones, and this turned out to be surprisingly easy to implement.

The site went live in February 2007; slowly the readers, and with them new oppo, began to trickle in. Obama had unpaid parking tickets from his days at Harvard Law School. Giuliani roomed with a gay couple after his separation from his second wife. Tommy Thompson had rumored affairs. Also, even more satisfying, I could tell from my server logs that OppoDepot was becoming a destination for seekers of dirt. I could see the search strings that brought them, streaming in like verse, an ongoing anti-ode to our tarnished political choices:

rudy giuliani cross dressing photos

bill richardson women crotch

carol shepp car accident

opposition research chuck hagel

hillary clinton and option trading

barack obama rezko swift boat

gov. richardson's obscene gesture

joe biden gaffe

brownback porn

chris dodd scandal

barney frank mike huckabee

bill richardson—leaking information

biden slave state quote

But true contagion proved elusive. Although in its first three weeks OppoDepot attracted roughly 100,000 hits from 5,000 visitors, these all came mostly in a very short spike at the beginning, which was followed immediately thereafter by a precipitous falloff:

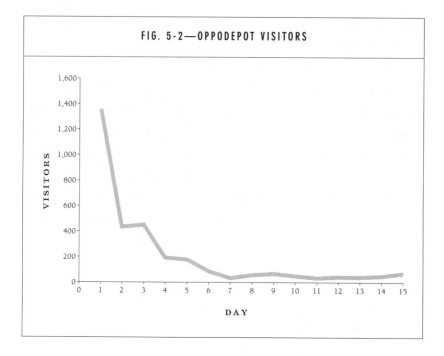

FIG. 5-2—OPPODEPOT VISITORS

Worse, the traffic did not translate into blog posts: by the end of the first month I had gotten only six. The experimental design had failed, I feared, and so I returned to the laboratory for more tests.

THE LONG TAIL OF TRUTH

In the months leading up to the 2004 presidential election, a team of neuroscientists at Emory University used a brain scanner to illuminate a dismal truth about the political mind. They recruited thirty strongly partisan subjects, half Democrats and half Republicans, and studied their reactions to political statements; specifically, to apparent contradictions on the part of political figures. Each subject was placed in an MRI scanner so that brain activity could be monitored while he or she was shown slides.

In each set of slides, the first showed an alleged quotation by a political figure; for example this quote, attributed to George W. Bush in

2000: "Ken Lay is a supporter of mine. . . . I plan to run the government like a CEO runs a company. Ken Lay and Enron are a model of how I'll do that." (In fact, Bush said no such thing: the quotes were all at least partially fabricated.) The second slide then showed a statement of supposed fact that contradicted the quote: e.g., "Mr. Bush now avoids any mention of Ken Lay and is critical of Enron when asked."

At this point, the subjects were asked to rate, on a scale of 1 to 4, how inconsistent the political figure's words were with the truth. After entering this rating, the subjects were then shown an ameliorating fact about the apparent inconsistency—e.g., "People who know the president report that he feels betrayed by Ken Lay, and was genuinely shocked to find that Enron's leadership had been corrupt"—and then asked again to rate, from 1 to 4, how inconsistent the figure's words and actions were.

The survey results were predictable: the subjects were far more likely to ascribe inconsistency to their opponents' candidate than to their own, even after considering the exculpatory evidence:

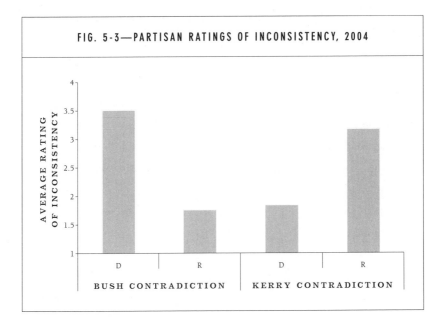

FIG. 5-3—PARTISAN RATINGS OF INCONSISTENCY, 2004

Far more striking, though, was what the Emory researchers saw on the brain scans. When these partisan subjects were "considering" whether the statements contradicted each other, the part of the brain associated with reasoning—the dorsolateral prefrontal cortex—was not being employed at all. Instead, a large region of activation was seen in the ventral stratum, indicating that the subjects' responses were essentially emotional—in fact, they were getting a tremendous psychological reward, as if they had solved a puzzle or won a bet. "None of the circuits involved in conscious reasoning were particularly engaged," the lead researcher, Drew Westen, told *Newsweek* in 2006 on announcing the findings. "Essentially, it appears as if partisans twirl the cognitive kaleidoscope until they get the conclusions they want, and then they get massively reinforced for it, with the elimination of negative emotional states and activation of positive ones."

What the Emory researchers had documented was simply the neurological correlate of a psychological phenomenon that has been observed for centuries. "The human understanding," wrote the philosopher Francis Bacon in his 1620 treatise *Novum Organum,*

> when it has once adopted an opinion (either as being the received opinion or as being agreeable to itself) draws all things else to support and agree with it. And though there be a greater number and weight of instances to be found on the other side, yet these it either neglects and despises, or else by some distinction sets aside and rejects; in order that by this great and pernicious predetermination the authority of its former conclusions may remain inviolate.

In the psychological literature, the tendency to disregard data that runs against held opinions is called *confirmation bias,* and its existence has been corroborated by study after study. This bias is not merely a political phenomenon, of course. Test-takers asked to give only supporting reasons for their conclusions will become more overconfident in their rightness. Gamblers will marshal evidence to explain away their losses as unlucky flukes, but ignore similar evidence about their wins. Consumers who have just made a major purchase will seek out evidence supporting their purchase while eschewing evidence against it. In short, we like to fill our minds with information that confirms what we already believe; this information in turn doubles down our already existing support of what we think or dismissal of what we disbelieve.

It is in this regard that the Internet and confirmation bias are conspiring to erode what remains of reasonable political discourse in this country. The mechanics of this dissolution are simple: first, the sheer quantity of media has reached the point where even the most assiduous news fan can consume an entire day's reading by simply ingesting only those tidbits that support his or her own views; and second, the network of political blogs, through a feedback loop among bloggers and readers, has evolved into a machine that supplies the reader exactly this prefiltered information. A vivid illustration of this latter point was made in 2005 by two researchers, Lada Adamic of HP Labs and Natalie Glance of Intelliseek, who had analyzed all the posts of the top twenty blogs of both political camps in the four months leading up to the 2004 election. In particular, they tracked how many times each blog linked to others on the list. What they found was that some 85 percent of the blogs' links were to other blogs on their own side, with almost no blog showing any particular respect for *any* blog on the other side. When they graphically represented the total citations, with lines representing five or more cross-citations between each node, it looked like this—

FIG. 5-4—ADAMIC AND GLANCE'S POLITICAL BLOG CLOUDS

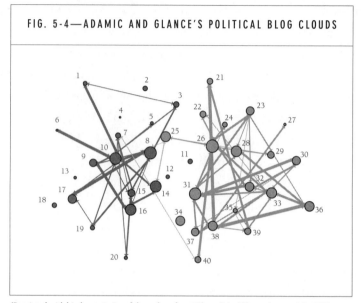

(Reprinted with kind permission of the authors from "The political blogosphere and the 2004 U.S. election: divided they blog," by L. A. Adamic and N. Glance, LinkKDD'05, Chicago, IL, pp. 36–43, 2005.)

—with the nodes 1 through 20 representing the left-wing blogs, 21 through 40 the right-wing blogs. When only connections of more than twenty-five posts are shown, communion between left and right disappears entirely. This represents no conspiracy among the bloggers, of course; they simply self-select what they read and post, and their self-selection tends, as is natural, toward that which supports their preexisting conclusions. Ideas of a feather flock together, and it has always been thus.

But the problem, once again, is speed. The Internet allows the like-minded to find one another so quickly, and with so little exposure to other points of view. Indeed, in this regard, the forward march of search technology threatens to balkanize our politics even further: the ability to ever more agilely find what we are looking for, while excluding the rest, is exactly what a citizen does not need in making his or her political choices. The phenomenon is parallel to Chris Anderson's "Long

Tail" idea as it pertains to commerce: the combination of nearly infinite inventory, on the one hand, and a national or even global customer base, on the other, means that Internet-based businesses can both satisfy consumers' most obscure tastes and make a profit doing so. For example, in the case of video stores, the limitations of geography and the cost of rent force Blockbuster stores to limit their selection only to broadly popular titles, whereas a delivery service like Netflix can stock at least one copy of literally every DVD ever released because their marginal cost of stocking each title is so low. What this means for culture, Anderson hopes, is a future where everything stays in print, always available, always profitable. "Abundant, cheap distribution," he writes, "means abundant, cheap, and unlimited variety."

In the realm of political discourse, and indeed of narrative in general, I fear we have fallen into a far less salutary situation. One might call it the Long Tail of Truth: given any trend that one wants to identify in the world—about the popularity of a buzzword or a band, the mendacity of a politician or a pundit, the rise or fall of any fashion—on the Internet one can readily convince oneself that the trend exists, as long as one runs the right targeted search or browses the properly biased sites. In the journalism world, there is a term for these sorts of cobbled-together narratives, which pluck anecdotes from the reporting of others in an attempt to prove a case: the "clip job." But of course that term harkens back to an era when the previous reporting had to be clipped out of physical publications, so the reporter would at least have been exposed to the context around each clipping—would have gotten, for example, a sense for how much time had elapsed between the instances. Today, clip jobs are accomplished with no clipping at all, but rather with directed searches on Nexis or Google, which present an instant, atemporalized buffet of anecdotes to fatten up whatever trend the journalist desires to see. And this is exactly the sort of "journalism" being plied by our entire nation of pundits today, from the lowliest blog all the way up to the TV anchor desk. With the Long Tail of Truth, telling ourselves new stories about ourselves has never been easier: abundant, cheap distribution of facts means an abundant, cheap, and unlimited variety of narratives, on demand, all the time.

OPPODEPOT PHASE TWO

This was precisely the use I had seen for OppoDepot: it would make the Long Tail of Truth even easier. Imagine the hypothetical reporter or blogger who decides he wants to tar a presidential candidate with a particular line of argument—as a coward, perhaps, or a fibber, or a peacenik. The writer could run a Google search with some relevant terms (*"barack obama" liar*) or read articles on the candidate from a sympathetic blog, and thereby maybe get the ammunition he needed: three (in the general rule) anecdotes about the candidates—i.e., nanostories—necessary to define a trend, QED. But OppoDepot would render all this searching and synthesis unnecessary. The blogger could simply visit the candidate's OppoDepot page and find precisely the nanostories he needed; such, at least, was the dream.

Why, then, had the site not taken off as expected? The problem, it occurred to me, might very well be the *lack* of partisanship on the OppoDepot site. As Adamic and Glance had demonstrated, Internet readers were accustomed to partisan echo chambers, and so they distrusted sites that played both sides. A few e-mailers to OppoDepot had made roughly this same point but in less scientific terms; "Wow, this site is so unbiased," one Ron Paul supporter had written, "I want to shit on it." I began to toy with a new hypothesis: that a political discourse so riven into rival camps might never embrace a bipartisan OppoDepot.

In order to test this notion, I developed a second phase of the experiment. First, I took out an advertising account with Google so I could buy some smear search terms: *"fred thompson lazy," "obama muslim," "hunter bribery,"* and scores more as well, making specific references to the nanostories around each of the candidates. Second, for the keywords about each candidate, I wrote up an ad that the Google searcher would see, inviting him or her to come see more dirt, e.g.:

> **Better Dead Than Fred**
> The truth about Fred Thompson, at
> Web 2.0's oppo research homepage—
> www.oppodepot.com

> **Dennis = Menace**
> Get the truth about Kucinich at
> Web 2.0's oppo research homepage—
> www.oppodepot.com

Third, I plotted out a schedule. For two weeks OppoDepot would continue to slur candidates of both parties. But for the two weeks after that, it would sully only Republican candidates; and for the two weeks after that, it would malign only Democratic candidates. During these partisan phases, I would run only the Google ads about the relevant candidates, and would double the overall ad buy in order not to skew the results.

Once the ads began to run, the traffic for the site steadily grew, and tips began to pour in. On Rudy Giuliani: *Retains on payroll a priest accused of child rape.* On Christopher Dodd: *Back in the 1990's he and Ted Kennedy were accused of grabbing and "sandwhiching" a D.C. waitress between them at a bar.* On Dennis Kucinich: *During this last election in 2004 . . . on one side of his campaign signs . . . he had "Re-elect Dennis" on the other sign it was done in Arabic.* On Ron Paul: *Ron Paul is older than John McCain.* And, of course, on Mitt Romney: *Mitt Romney treated his dog cruelly during a family vacation.*

But to my surprise, when I made the site partisan, the traffic began to drop off—a little bit when it was an anti-Republican site, and then a lot when it became an anti-Democrat site:

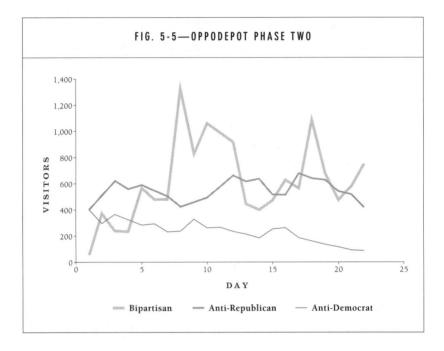

FIG. 5-5—OPPODEPOT PHASE TWO

The volatility of the bipartisan site was far greater, but the average daily traffic was markedly higher: 617 visitors per day versus 546 for the anti-Republican version and 297 for the anti-Democrat version. And, of course, none of these outcomes could by any stretch of the imagination be called "viral." All told, I had spent more than $2,200 on Google ads, plus a few hundred more for web hosting, to attract 38,000 visitors in total—less than a quarter of what the Right-Wing *New York Times*, which netted me $2,500, had gotten for free. I had intended to find out if I could make American politics any more cynical; but from where I now sat, thousands of dollars poorer and the owner of an unpopular repository of political dirt, the most cynical person in American politics was apparently me.

VOTE THE SAME

Rather than wallow in the despondency that is the failed meme-maker's inevitable lot, I decided to pay a visit to Jonah Peretti. His start-up, BuzzFeed, had since been funded and launched, and it had set up offices in Chinatown on an open, smartly renovated floor just above an illegal Chinese gambling parlor. At a computer monitor he showed me around the BuzzFeed site, which zeroed in on new trends in online conversation by crawling thousands of blogs and analyzing them using a technology called "acceleration detection"—i.e., the search for ramped-up attention. When the site's editors saw interesting connections pop up on the trend detector, they would then write them up as items in a humorously ironic style. The week I visited, new "trends" included "Inarticulate White People" (after minor gaffes by Mitt Romney and John McCain), "Girl-on-Girl Feel-Ups" (linking a number of minor incidents involving female celebrities), "Husbands Taking Their Wives' Names" (after a *USA Today* article on the subject sparked some online conversation), and "Shower Caps" (after the rapper Snoop Dogg took to wearing one out and about). Browsing through the BuzzFeed archives was already an enjoyable stroll through a cultural graveyard: the headstones of trends birthed and then left to perish.

For my part, I showed him OppoDepot, and I could tell by his face that he knew it was a hopeless case. Quite charitably he declined to say so, and he helpfully suggested some skullduggery I might employ to turn the situation around. For example, I could change candidates' Wikipedia entries and justify my changes with links to the OppoDepot site. I could post Craigslist listings for jobs—e.g., "Looking for database programmer; fun environment to work in"—on employment boards, which might drive curious would-be applicants to view the site. Or, Jonah said, "you could create false rumors. You could have one of the candidates' pages be filled with real softballs—and then spread the rumor that that candidate created the site." They were inspired suggestions, but I knew that they couldn't possibly work. There was something about the political climate that OppoDepot had misgauged.

That very week, it so happened, Jonah had helped the Huffington Post unmask the maker of the biggest political meme of the moment: an anti–Hillary Clinton video on YouTube that was an homage to Apple Computer's famous "1984" advertisement. Posted by an anonymous YouTube user named ParkRidge47, the sophisticated ad (entitled "Vote Different") depicted an Obama supporter crashing through a Big Brother–type screen bearing Hillary Clinton's dour visage. The video had accumulated some 500,000 views, and speculation as to the maker's identity had found its way into scores of newspapers and television shows. "This is a historic shift from a world in which a few important media outlets kind of control the dialogue to a game where anyone can play," noted Howard Kurtz, the CNN host and media critic for the *Washington Post*. It was at the height of the controversy when the Huffington Post, in a remarkable reporting coup, suddenly announced that it had identified the man who made the ad. (Jonah declined to give specific details, other than saying he "did a little bit of cybersleuthing" and made "some phone calls.")

The ad had been made by Phil de Vellis, who—as I had expected—was hardly the portrait of a starry-eyed amateur: a technology consultant at Blue State Digital, a prominent Democratic web-strategy firm, de Vellis had previously served as the Internet communications director for the successful 2006 Senate bid of Sherrod Brown (D–Ohio). To those who followed that race closely, de Vellis was notorious as a classic Internet-era political operative. He had been widely suspected of planting abusive pro-Brown propaganda in the comments boards of sites supporting Paul Hackett, an Iraq war veteran and netroots favorite who was Brown's main competitor in the Democratic primary. (Comments from the sites were traced back to the same Internet address as de Vellis's, though he denied involvement.) He had been caught e-mailing anti-Hackett talking points to right-wing bloggers—normal bare-knuckle politics, to be sure, but a clear breach of Democratic loyalty. Given a chance to explain his anti-Hillary ad by the Huffington Post, de Vellis tried to wrap his actions in just the sort of gauzy populist sentiment that the mainstream media wanted. "I made the 'Vote Different' ad," he wrote,

> because I wanted to express my feelings about the Democratic primary, and because I wanted to show that an individual citizen can affect the process. There are thousands of other people who could have made this ad, and I guarantee that more ads like it—by people of all political persuasions—will follow.
>
> This shows that the future of American politics rests in the hands of ordinary citizens.

But such bromides did nothing to deter the backlash. Blue State Digital was doing consulting work for Obama, and even though de Vellis protested (plausibly, given that his firm was working for two of the other candidates as well) that his work on the ad had been kept secret from both his colleagues and the campaign, the media pounced. Obama was forced into denials that he had known anything about it. De Vellis resigned from his firm. It all felt very much like 2004 politics, except in video instead of in print. It was OppoDepot with better production values.

"Everyone is so hyped about YouTube," Jonah told me, in trying to explain why the ad had been a big story. "There is this idea that YouTube will be the way blogs were the last election." But based on the "Vote Different" ad, I couldn't see how it was any different at all.

SONGS OF THEMSELVES

It was nearly eight more months before YouTube offered up a video that proved to me how wrong I was. In late October 2007, after the film star Chuck Norris wrote an online column (on the Christian site WorldNet Daily) endorsing the former Arkansas governor Mike Huckabee for president, the campaign met with Norris and tried to brainstorm ways to get the two men together in some sort of advertisement. Through his young son, Huckabee media consultant Bob Wickers had heard about ChuckNorrisFacts.com, a widely contagious website that, in keeping with Norris's tough-guy persona, ascribes to him surprising powers, e.g.: "When Chuck Norris does a pushup, he isn't lifting himself up, he's pushing the Earth down." Or: "There is no theory of evolution. Just a list of creatures Chuck Norris has allowed to live." Or: "There is no chin behind Chuck Norris' beard. There is only another fist." Given that Norris's film career had peaked in roughly 1986, it is barely an exaggeration to say that an entire generation of Internet users had come to know the martial-arts star *just* through the Chuck Norris Facts website.

Out of the memetic convergence between Norris and Huckabee was a Internet success story born. Chip Saltsman, Huckabee's national campaign manager, explained to a Tennessee business magazine how it came together. "Bob [Wickers] and I started brainstorming in the Surf Ballroom, of all places"—the classic Iowa venue where Buddy Holly and Ritchie Valens played their final concert in 1959 before perishing in a plane crash—"and we got Chuck's office on the phone. And one of the ideas we had was maybe to do some Chuck Norris facts and then some Mike Huckabee facts." Saltsman and Huckabee flew to visit Norris in Texas, and on the plane Saltsman came up with the line that Huckabee would use to open the ad. "My plan to secure the border? Two words: Chuck Norris."

For $60,000, the campaign produced a minute-long online ad that within a few weeks amassed over 1,500,000 views on YouTube. Arguably the ad was responsible for catapulting Mike Huckabee from the second tier of Republican candidates into the first, as Americans were for the first time encouraged to look past the governor's overwhelmingly right-wing policies to witness his not inconsiderable comedic gifts. Despite the success of "Vote Different," I would argue that "Chuck Norris Approved" (as the video was officially called) served as the opening salvo of an online 2008 campaign that really was defined by YouTube more than by blogs. The difference was clear not just in how the ad employed a universal comedy instead of a politically charged critique. It was that Huckabee's ad used Chuck Norris more for his microcelebrity than for his celebrity—i.e., by using Chuck Norris Facts, it presented the actor not as a mere celebrity endorser but as an online touchstone, and so his ad immediately became an eager, self-aware contribution to the Internet it-child scrum.

In 2004, online politics had felt almost like a throwback to the attack politics of the late eighteenth and early nineteenth centuries, when the availability of inexpensive printing technology allowed small publishers, and their often scurrilous political attacks, to thrive. Blogs were like this old anarchic print culture, fostering ideology, argument, and a sort of team cohesion based on enmity. With YouTube in 2008, it suddenly seemed as if nearly two centuries had sped by and we were in the early decades of television, when ideological lines were massaged over by the overwhelming force of *personality*. Seen through a 2004 prism, Hillary Clinton's candidacy looked inevitable, because her entire political profile was calculated to win a hyperpartisan war of ideology and argument, smears and countersmears: hated by her enemies, defended to the teeth by her allies, funded and staffed to the hilt by battle-tested meme warriors, no other candidate was better equipped to handle what the right-wing Luftwaffe would inevitably drop on her.

But by 2008, Clinton looked like Richard Nixon in 1960, a hard political creature in a time of telegenic youth and charisma. Online video
was tilting the conversation toward the likeable candidates (Obama,
Huckabee, and to a certain extent McCain), toward their famous en-
dorsers (such as Norris, or the pop star will.i.am who made the season's
most successful YouTube ad, the celebrity-studded "Yes We Can" music
video)—and, moreover, toward any upbeat fan who made his or her
own videos, winning over audiences with sheer enthusiasm.

Obama, in particular, was the sort of candidate whom people wanted
to be seen performing *for*. One especially pleasing example: in a Democratic primary dominated by a high-profile fight for the Latino vote,
perhaps the most strategically brilliant YouTube video was devised by
Miguel Orozco, a Mexican-American media consultant in Los Angeles.
Orozco had created (on his own, not on the campaign's behalf) a
site called "Amigos de Obama," attempting to reach out to Spanish-
speaking voters. The site's first offering was an MP3 of a pro-Obama
song in the "reggaeton" style (a blend of reggae and Latin dance music).
But later, as the decisive Texas primary was approaching, Orozco hit
upon an even better idea. He decided to write a pro-Obama song in the
corrido style, a mariachi ballad that by tradition tells the story of a great
man—a form still used to this day by Mexican politicians, especially
in rural areas. More than 200,000 people watched Orozco's utterly
winning video, in which a decked-out Mexican band walks the streets
of an anonymous city, singing out to their candidate:

Al candidato quien es Barack Obama,
Este corrido le canto con el alma,
Humilde fue nacido tambien sin pretencion,
Emprezo por las calles de Chicago,
Trabajando pa' lograr una vision,
Pa' proteger la gente trabajadora,
Y traernos todo juntos,

En esta gran nacion,
¡Viva Obama! (¡Viva!) ¡Viva Obama! (¡Viva!)
Familias unidas, seguras y hasta,
Con plan de salud*

Around the same time, in Naperville, Illinois, a twelve-year-old boy was finding fans for a different sort of *corrido*. When Chaz Yario sang a song to Obama in his science class, he landed in detention. So he videotaped himself singing the song in front of an American flag, put the video on YouTube, and accompanied it with a note: "I got a detention for singing this song in class so i need your help. I want to meet obama so he can sign my detention slip the more people you send it to the more likely it will get back to barack. thsnk 4 your help. Enjoy!!" The song was called "Hey There Obama" (a goof on "Hey There Delilah," then a popular song by a band called the Plain White T's), and it was a spare, mournful acoustic number:

Hey there Obama
What's it like in Washington, D.C.?
You want to be the president
And that would make history
Yes it would
I think you should be the president

---

* *Translation:*
To the candidate who is Barack Obama
I sing this corrido with all my soul
He was born humble without pretension
He began in the streets of Chicago
Working to achieve a vision
To protect the working people
And bring us all together in this great nation
Viva Obama! Viva Obama!
Families united and safe and even with a health care plan

Yes you should
I know that you could

. . .

Barack Obama superstar
Bet you have a nice car
Oh forget Hillary
I watch you on the TV
Oh it's time for democracy
And you will win probably
Will win probably

Watching Chaz's video, which at this writing had gotten more than 160,000 views, it became apparent just how doomed Hillary Clinton's campaign was, at least in the annals of popular culture. Obama had become the sort of celebrity that a gawky, twelve-year-old white boy could become cool just by association with him.

The best online video of the 2008 primary season was a product of incredible serendipity. Outside a Democratic debate in Hollywood, an amateur videographer ambushed an Obama supporter and began to press him on the candidate's programs. The supporter was young and black, and wore a baseball cap and a choker necklace made of shells; his interlocutor, off camera, took a hectoring tone, his voice seemingly older, slightly nasal. "So why are you for Obama?" the older man asks on the video, and at first the young man seems to stumble.

"Because I feel like he is—the best qualified candidate. I think that he's got an excellent chance to win, especially against McCain. I think that he—"

The off-camera voice cuts in. "Why is he the best qualified?"

"Well, I feel like he's a person who actually represents a positive change in society and who can bring together a broad swath of people—"

"How is he doing that, specifically? Do you have any *specifics*?"

But slowly, as the two men parry over the course of a five-minute conversation, the Obama supporter—who in fact was a ringer of sorts, a Harvard-educated musician and media activist named Derrick Ashong—turns the tables on his questioner, overwhelming him with precisely the specifics the viewer has feared he doesn't possess. "With Obama's program," Ashong says, his once-laconic tone growing ever more engaged, more pointed, "we have subsidies for people who can't afford to pay, and that is something that we don't have now. . . . I don't think that we want to create a market for health care per se. We don't want futures traded in health care, for example. I think that we've got to be more measured in how we approach it. Because we don't want to leave people out. You're going to have all kind of rising costs if people don't actually get access to health care." Now it is Ashong who will not let his interlocutor get a word in edgewise. "The other thing is, we've got so much, like—secondary health care, we don't have preventative care? We would save tons of money if we actually invested in keeping people healthy in the first place!"

By the end, Ashong is in total command, as he bids to convert his (now genuinely impressed) interviewer to Obama's cause. When the questioner doubts how much a president can really do ("Congress makes the laws," he points out), Ashong moves in for the sale.

"I'm *so* glad you asked that," he says. "That's the key thing. And this is why I support Obama over Clinton. I feel like Clinton is too partisan. In order to make this happen, you've got to have [leaders] who are willing to pursue the national interest instead of just their party's interest."

The video had a clear metaphorical resonance, one that explains, I think, the overwhelming appeal it had for the one million people who would view it on YouTube in the weeks after its release. To Obama's nervous fans, Ashong embodied a sort of stand-in for the candidate himself, and through his response under pressure he salved some of our fears about Obama. Here was a young, charismatic supporter who proved himself, against all prejudices and fears, a man of almost unbelievable substance, and succeeded—as we hoped Obama would—in not only countering the worst of what an enemy threw at him but making that enemy, implausibly, a friend. The video was a five-minute daydream of how the general-election campaign (and an Obama administration) would go.

There was another metaphor that struck me, though: I could not help but think about the video as an allegory for the Internet-era conversation as a whole, for how it might clamber up out of the murk somewhat, past the petty meme warfare, past the empty enthusiasms for microcelebrity, and past, even, the urge to manufacture meaningless nanostories. Derrick Ashong had not rushed to play pundit but was instead a patient advocate, waiting to hear out his opposition before launching a counterattack. He had immersed himself in facts but kept his mind open about their interpretation. His goal was a pragmatic one: he deployed both his charm and his arguments not to stir up sensation but to change a mind and win a vote. The question is whether enough of us will care to follow his example.

CONCLUSION

NOTES FOR
FURTHER RESEARCH

Early in the general election, Obama's campaign unveiled a novel strategic weapon in its war against nanostories. Called FightTheSmears .com, it was a website that gathered together all the most scurrilous, contagious rumors about the candidate and supplied specific rebuttals to each. That Michelle Obama had said "whitey" at a public event; that Barack's birth certificate had gone missing, or was a forgery; that he was actually a Muslim; that he had refused to say the Pledge of Allegiance— all these false statements, which had spread for months through chain e-mails and right-wing websites, were aired and refuted on the campaign's new site. It is unclear how successful this effort actually was, of course, considering how much these and other smears dogged Obama up until Election Day.* But the strategic appeal of Fight the Smears was

---

* Indeed, the site may even have done harm: as the science writer Farhad Manjoo pointed out, all research on myths indicates that "repeating a claim, even if only

undeniable. The site was the equivalent of a Google bomb, in that its debunkings soon showed up in the top results for any search (e.g., *obama muslim*) made by any skeptical voter. And for dealing with the press—which tends to fuel nanostories by asking the candidates for comment, and then printing their denials as news, further propagating the story—the site was a master stroke, in that it allowed Obama and his handlers to respond to rumors without doing so on air. *Check the website,* they could tell reporters, right before changing the subject.

Personally, I could not regard FightTheSmears.com as anything other than a shameless violation of my intellectual property. For what was the site if not OppoDepot, except distilled down to a single candidate and turned on its head? The reversal made perfect sense, really, once I saw the principle at work. To see all these nanostories lumped together, *as* nanostories, somehow defused them, made them more mundane. Alongside one another they all seemed unconvincing and small. And that, to a certain extent, has been my own goal in writing this book: to consider political smears, and meaningless fads, and perishable bands, and momentary celebrities, and disposable narratives in general, as all objects in the same class, as species in the same low family of invertebrates. When herded together, the extent to which they have overrun our culture becomes clear. We love our nanostories, their birth and death thrill us, and yet we know that they are devouring us. We want reason in our politics, greatness in our art, and we see that these are incompatible with our feckless, churning conversation. We must learn how to neuter our nanostories, or at least to cut off their food supply.

---

to refute it, increases its apparent truthfulness." For example, three days after Norbert Schwarz, a psychologist at the University of Michigan, showed subjects a CDC flyer attempting to dispel myths about the flu vaccine, he found that his subjects misremembered, on average, 40 percent of the false statements as being true. So just by writing this paragraph as I did, listing the anti-Obama smears, I likely spread misinformation among at least a few readers. Apologies.

During my own years adventuring in viral culture, all the meme-makers I met were on some level trying to engineer a fix for this problem, the dilemma of disposability—the curse of the nanostory, the spike, the terror of the abandonment that inevitably follows the rush of viral blowup. And the approach arrived at by each was one that I, at some time or another, came to try on for myself. Like Jonah Peretti, the memetic engineer extraordinaire, I by and large approached meme-making with the remove of the social scientist, who can thereby explain away his projects' abandonment or even outright failure as more experimental data. Like John Harris of *The Politico*, Henry Cowling of the Viral Factory, or any of the countless other can-do viral entrepreneurs of the Web 2.0 boom, I have felt the temptation toward making memes for profit, toward learning to love the viral hive-mind whose whims, once detected by way of "most e-mailed" lists, MySpace friending, or Digg voting, can be continuously placated in exchange for hits and dollars. I also, at various times, have harbored a techno-utopian fondness for the meme machine, and I even have felt tempted, like *Time*'s "You" issue, to lionize viral culture as a people-powered paradise. But I also have seen the day-by-day destructiveness of the Internet churn, of the manufacture of nanostories with little regard for their ultimate truth. And like Kurt Strahm, even, the former painter and now Accidental Oracle, I have in my dark hours understood the personal allure, in the face of all this disposability, of receding into cynical monasticism, of conceiving meta-ideas but never executing them and thereby risking nothing.

So: how to sap the machine of its tyrannical power? For most of us, disengaging entirely from our communications technology is hardly desirable—or even possible, for that matter, if we are unwilling to lose our jobs and slide into Luddite penury in some far-off yurt. There are promising half measures, however, and some of them are being tried. Jake Silverstein, a writer and editor in Austin, has advocated for the celebration of "Internet Ramadan," a monthlong annual holiday when all Internet use is forbidden during the daytime. Along similar lines, the cookbook writer Mark Bittman recently wrote in the *New York Times* about his attempts at a "Secular Sabbath," a twenty-four-hour period each week when all electronic communication devices are to be powered off. The computing giant Intel has been experimenting with "Quiet Time" on Tuesday mornings, where employees are encouraged to go entirely offline, post DO NOT DISTURB signs on their doors, and give over four straight hours to the decadent pursuit of uninterrupted thought.

The hope is that by cordoning off spaces in our lives away from information, we will less often fall prey to our obsession with short-term thinking and the ephemeral narratives that accompany it. One is reminded of Nassim Taleb's fictional dentist who, when he reads his stock reports less often, paradoxically becomes better informed. By the same principle, we would be far better off reading our blogs daily instead of hourly, watching the news weekly instead of daily, looking for new bands and books and trends monthly (or even yearly) instead of weekly. For a particularly extreme corrective on this subject, we can look to the Long Now Foundation, a Bay Area–based group whose mission is to foster thinking on a 10,000-year time horizon. Established in 1996 (or, as the group puts it, 01996, the leading zero having been added "to solve the deca-millennium bug which will come into effect in about 8,000 years"), Long Now is laboring on two flagship projects—first, an ultra-accurate clock, to be built on a Nevada mountain, which will keep perfect time for at least ten millennia; and second, the Rosetta Project, designed to collect a permanent and exhaustive record of all 2,300 existing human languages, before any more of them die out. Danny Hillis, the group's cofounder, uses a vivid historical example to demonstrate how long-term thinking can work. "I think of the oak beams in the ceiling of College Hall at New College, Oxford," he wrote in a 1995 *Wired* essay about the clock project. He went on:

Last century, when the beams needed replacing, carpenters used oak trees that had been planted in 1386 when the dining hall was first built. The 14th-century builder had planted the trees in anticipation of the time, hundreds of years in the future, when the beams would need replacing. Did the carpenters plant new trees to replace the beams again a hundred years from now?

For consumers of art and culture, one simple way to sift out ephemerality is "time-shifting"—i.e., delaying one's experience of a cultural product long enough that any undue hype surrounding it has dissipated. In 2005, I came across an especially delightful example of time-shifting firsthand, when I told a new acquaintance what magazine I worked for. It was his favorite magazine, he replied with some excitement; indeed it was the only magazine he allowed himself to read. In fact, his devotion was such that he never missed a single page of any issue. Time being lamentably short, however, he was unable to get through an issue every month. And so he had devised a system: he kept his issues of the magazine sequentially on the shelf of his closet, adding each new issue to the right side while continuing to read the old copies in order from the left side.

What issue are you reading now? I asked him.

"Sometime in 1998," he said.

This, I realized, was the highest compliment he could possibly have paid to my magazine—if not to me personally, seeing as how I had not even been hired until 2000. He was picking up seven-year-old issues of a periodical and finding them relevant enough to read. *If you love something, set it free,* the old adage goes, on the principle that the object of requited affection will inevitably return. Time-shifting poses a sort of corollary for art: *If you want to see whether something is great, leave it on a shelf for seven days, or seven years, or seventy.* Technology, in this regard, can become a friend instead of a foe. TiVo permits one to put off television shows until one is ready to watch them. Netflix allows one to forgo movies in the theater and instead wait for the best on DVD. Amazon's formidable collection of small used-book sellers allows us to buy old and even out-of-print books as easily as buying new. If we cannot hope to overcome the pull of the now, we can at least attempt, as best we can, to see it alongside the *then*.

More generally: we must become judicious controllers of our own contexts, making careful and self-reflective choices about what we read, watch, consume. This is especially paramount for those of us who want not merely to enjoy art and culture but to create our own. The philosopher Friedrich Nietzsche drew a distinction between two ancient schools of thought, the Stoic and the Epicurean, in terms of their opposite solutions to the filtering of life experience. "The Epicurean," he wrote, "selects the situation, the persons, and even the events that suit his extremely irritable intellectual constitution; he gives up all others, which means almost everything, because they would be too strong and heavy for him to digest. The Stoic, on the other hand, trains himself to swallow stones and worms, slivers of glass and scorpions without nausea; he wants his stomach to become ultimately indifferent to whatever accidents of existence might pour into it."

Nietzsche goes on to say that while Stoicism might be a wise choice for "those who live in violent ages [or] depend on mercurial people," Epicureanism is always advisable for "anyone who foresees more or less that fate permits him to spin *a long thread*." Paring down one's own context, he says, is "what those have always done whose work is of the spirit"—*alle Menschen der geistigen Arbeit,* which in a footnote Nietzsche's translator and biographer Walter Kaufmann takes to signify "artists, scholars, writers."

If the road of the Stoic, he who would bear all burdens, absorb all information, was ever truly possible, it is no longer so today. We are all Epicureans now, whether we know it or not, because we each have access to far more inputs than we could ever possibly process. We all choose our own informational contexts today; the only question is how judiciously we choose. And so what we need is an ethos of responsible Epicureanism by which we forbid ourselves to live in entirely harmonious, self-selected fantasy worlds, on the one hand, or in controversy-crazed, novelty-driven data gluts on the other. David Levy, a professor at the University of Washington, has coined the term "information environmentalism" to describe the consciousness we need to foster, and the metaphor is a perfect one. We can no longer believe that our informational context is an infinite, incorruptible resource, a wellspring we can take for granted, an ecosystem we can never permanently pollute. But neither can we stop living within our data streams, shaping them and using them in our daily lives. So we must discover more sustainable approaches to information, to novelty, to storytelling. We cannot unplug the machine, nor would we want to; but we must rewire it to serve us, rather than the other way around. And for that, we must learn how to partially unplug ourselves.

ACKNOWLEDGMENTS

Thanks are due

—to the co-conspirators: Brian Spinks, Christian Lorentzen, Eugene
Mirman, Dan Goldstein, and Genevieve Smith, each of whom
had a hand in one or more of the experiments;

—to the early readers: Ben Austen, Jeff Sharlet, Julia Rabig, John
Williams, and Bryant Urstadt, who slogged through manuscripts
of this book and offered indispensable advice;

—to the staff of *Harper's Magazine*: Luke Mitchell, Roger Hodge,
Ellen Rosenbush, Lewis Lapham, Rick MacArthur, Ted Ross, and
all my other colleagues during a decade there;

—to Paul Reyes, Marc Smirnoff, and Michael Fitzgerald of *The
Oxford American*;

—to the whole crew of Viking, including Wendy Wolf, Lindsay Pre-
vette, Liz Parker, Jennifer Wang, and Daniel Lagin;

—and, most of all, to those without whom this book could not have
been written: Josh Kendall, Tina Bennett, Ben Metcalf, Monica
Murphy, Monica Murphy, Monica Murphy.

INDEX